Schiz

MW00639370

Disorder Simplified

Martine Daniel

chipmunkapublishing

the mental health publisher

Martine Daniel

Published by

Chipmunkapublishing

PO Box 6872

Brentwood

Essex CM13 1ZT

United Kingdom

http://www.chipmunkapublishing.com

Chipmunkapublishing gratefully acknowledge the support of Arts Council England.

Disclaimer

The information in this book has been compiled by way of general guidance in relation to schizoaffective disorder but is not a substitute for and not to be relied on for medical healthcare, pharmaceutical or other professional advice on specific circumstances and in specific locations. Please consult your GP or other medical practitioner before changing, stopping or starting any medical treatment. So far as the author is aware, all information given is correct and up to date as of September 2010. Practice, laws and regulations change and the reader should obtain up to date professional advice on any such issues. The author and publishers disclaim, as far as the law allows, any liability arising directly or indirectly from the use or misuse of the information contained in this book.

Martine Daniel

About the Author

Martine Daniel was born in York in 1981, and always dreamed of being a published author. Despite suffering mental health difficulties herself, her hopes of seeing her name in print never dimmed, and her dreams came true when her first novel, The Fire in Your Eyes, was published by Chipmunka Publishing in 2009.

Martine hopes that by bringing the experience of mental illness alive in her works of fiction she can contribute to the on-going battle to reduce the stigma surrounding mental health issues.

Schizoaffective Disorder Simplified is her first work of non-fiction.

You can find out more about Martine Daniel on her website www.martinedaniel.co.uk.

Martine Daniel

Contents

Restlessness and agitation
Becoming more talkative
Trying to achieve unrealistic goals
Forgetting to eat
Taking risks and acting impulsively
Irritability and aggressiveness
Heightened senses
Increased self-confidence and self-importance
Increased sensitivity
Racing thoughts
Muddled thinking
Having lots of ideas

What is it like to be manic?
Manic Moments

Chapter Three: Depression and Mixed States

What is depression?

What is atypical depression?

Symptoms of depression in more depth
Not being able to feel
Not caring about anything
Losing interest and motivation
Feeling tired and drained of energy
Feeling worse at particular times of the day
Feeling worthless
Feeling guilty
Becoming more sensitive
Irritability
Feeling hopeless and helpless
Feeling worried and anxious
Feeling lethargic
Withdrawal and avoidance
Thinking negatively
Sluggish thoughts

What is a mixed state?

Depression Alliance

Depression UK (D-UK)

Samaritans

MDF: the bipolar organisation

Carers UK

Mental Health Foundation

Introduction

Schizoaffective disorder is a condition that many people have never heard of, and yet it affects as many as 1 in every 200 people – that's 0.5% of the population. Surprisingly, there are very few books about schizoaffective disorder available, and many of those that are available are expensive medical textbooks not aimed at the general reader.

This book aims to simplify schizoaffective disorder and make the information about the disorder accessible to all. You may be reading this because you have been given a diagnosis of schizoaffective disorder, because a friend or family member has schizoaffective disorder, or because you just have a healthy interest in mental health issues. Either way, I hope that this book will answer all the questions you have about schizoaffective disorder, including what it is, how it is treated, and how to cope with the illness.

Martine Daniel

Chapter One: Introducing Schizoaffective Disorder

What is schizoaffective disorder?

Most people will have heard of mental illnesses such as schizophrenia and bipolar disorder (formerly known as manic depression) but you could be forgiven for never having heard about schizoaffective disorder. Schizoaffective disorder is less common than schizophrenia and bipolar disorder and it is an often misunderstood condition.

Schizoaffective disorder is a serious mental illness that can have profoundly disrupting effects on people's lives. It is closely related to both schizophrenia and bipolar disorder and shares symptoms with both the disorders. It was once thought that people with schizoaffective disorder were actually experiencing an unlucky coincidence of the two conditions. Now, however, schizoaffective disorder is recognised as an illness in its own right.

Schizoaffective disorder can easily be confused with bipolar disorder and schizophrenia because the symptoms are very similar. Someone with schizoaffective disorder will generally experience the hallucinations and delusions that are commonly associated with schizophrenia at the same time as, or within a few days of, experiencing the mood disturbances of mania or depression that are usually associated with bipolar disorder.

Statistically, around one in every two hundred people (0.5% of the population) will develop schizoaffective disorder at some point in their lives. This figure, however, may not be accurate, because many people with schizoaffective disorder are mistakenly diagnosed with either schizophrenia or bipolar disorder. This is because it is often difficult for psychiatrists to distinguish between the three conditions, particularly in the early stages of assessment. It can often take many months, or even years, for a correct diagnosis to be given.

What are the symptoms of schizoaffective disorder?

The symptoms of schizoaffective disorder include *psychotic symptoms*, such as hallucinations, delusions and thought disorder, and *affective symptoms*, such as hypomania, mania, depression and mixed states.

The symptoms of schizoaffective disorder are very similar to the symptoms of bipolar disorder with psychosis, which is one of the reasons the condition is so difficult to diagnose. The main difference between schizoaffective disorder and bipolar disorder with psychosis is that people with schizoaffective disorder will experience the psychotic symptoms *outside* of a mood episode as well as during a mood episode, whereas someone with bipolar disorder will experience hallucinations and delusions only *during* a mood episode.

Part one of this book explains the symptoms of schizoaffective disorder in more depth.

Who gets schizoaffective disorder, and when do they get it?

Schizoaffective disorder can affect anyone, but generally more women than men tend to suffer from the illness. The illness often begins in late adolescence or early adulthood, with a typical age of onset of between 16 and 30. Some people, however, will start with the illness earlier or later in their lifetime.

Are there different types of schizoaffective disorder?

There are two different types of schizoaffective disorder: bipolar type and depressive type. As their names suggest, the bipolar type involves affective (mood) symptoms of mania and depression as well as psychosis, whilst the depressive type involves depression and psychosis but not mania.

What is the prognosis for people with schizoaffective disorder?

The prognosis for people with schizoaffective disorder is largely dependent on the form of the illness (depressive or bipolar type) and the presence or absence of a trigger. If there is a major life event as a prompting stressor, or an unusual traumatic experience preceded the occurrence of the disorder, chances of a more favourable outcome are higher. If there is not a particular triggering event, the outcome is less likely to be positive.

The bipolar form of the disorder tends to respond better to treatment than the depressive form. Generally, the earlier the disorder is identified and treated, and the fewer lapses from taking medications, the more positive the outcome.

What causes schizoaffective disorder?

Although the exact causes of schizoaffective disorder aren't known, it is thought that the illness is caused by a combination of genetic and environmental factors.

According to mental health charity Rethink[1], there is evidence that there is some kind of chemical imbalance in neurotransmitters (the chemical messengers of the brain) in people with schizoaffective disorder. It is unclear yet whether the chemical imbalance is down to environmental factors or genetic factors.

---

[1]

http://www.rethink.org/about_mental_illness/mental_ill nesses_and_disorders/schizoaffective_disorder/causes_of_sc hizoaffe.html

Genetic factors

Schizoaffective disorder tends to occur more in families where there is a history of schizoaffective disorder, schizophrenia, or bipolar disorder. This implies that there is a genetic predisposition towards developing the illness, although there isn't yet one single gene that has been definitively identified as being the cause of mental illness.

Environmental Factors

One major cause of schizoaffective disorder seems to be stress. Stress can not only trigger initial episodes of illness but it is often also responsible for triggering subsequent episodes of illness. It is therefore important for people with schizoaffective disorder to live in an environment with as little stress as possible, and to identify the particular types of stress that can trigger episodes.

How is schizoaffective disorder diagnosed?

The diagnosis of schizoaffective disorder lies entirely in a psychiatrist's hands. There are no blood tests or brain scans that can establish the diagnosis with absolute certainty.

A psychiatrist will make a diagnosis by interviewing the person in great detail. The interview may last an hour or more, and involve questions about the person's symptoms and their life history. Often a psychiatrist will talk to other people who know the person well, especially if the person is psychotic, because it can be difficult to get answers from someone in the acute stages of psychosis. Psychiatrists will observe the person's behaviour, too, during the course of the assessment as there are certain types of behaviour that are characteristic of schizoaffective disorder.

A diagnosis of schizoaffective disorder is made according to one of two sets of criteria, the American DSM-IV (TR) or the World Health Organisation's ICD-10. These criteria help to differentiate schizoaffective disorder from bipolar disorder and schizophrenia. It can sometimes take months or even years for the person to receive the correct diagnosis if their symptoms don't match the criteria enough for a firm diagnosis to be made.

One of the main ways psychiatrists distinguish schizoaffective disorder from schizophrenia and bipolar disorder is in the timing of the symptoms. An episode of schizoaffective disorder needs to last for at least a month and the affective symptoms and the psychotic symptoms should be happening at the same time or within a few days of each other. To complicate matters further, for two weeks out of the month, the affective symptoms should disappear so that only the psychotic symptoms remain.

See appendices one and two for the DSM-IV (TR) and ICD-10 diagnostic criteria for schizoaffective disorder.

How is schizoaffective disorder treated?

Schizoaffective disorder is usually treated with a combination of medication and therapy. Medications used to treat schizoaffective disorder include anti-psychotics, anti-depressants, mood stabilisers and anti-anxiety medications. Therapy may include cognitive behavioural therapy, family therapy and creative therapies.

For more details on the treatment of schizoaffective disorder, see part two: treatment.

What is the risk of suicide in schizoaffective disorder?

Between 30% and 40% of people with schizoaffective disorder attempt suicide at some point during the course of their illness. 10% of this number will succeed in their attempts to kill themselves.

What other conditions do people commonly have with schizoaffective disorder?

Schizoaffective disorder can occur together with several other disorders. This is commonly called comorbidity. Some of the common comorbid problems that occur with schizoaffective disorder are:

- Alcohol and drug problems
- Anxiety
- Panic disorder with agoraphobia
- Panic disorder without agoraphobia
- Specific phobia
- Social phobia
- Obsessive compulsive disorder
- Generalised anxiety disorder

PART ONE:

SYMPTOMS of
SCHIZOAFFECTIVE DISORDER

Martine Daniel

Chapter Two: Mania and Hypomania

Mania and hypomania are common symptoms for people with the bipolar type of schizoaffective disorder.

What is mania?

Mania is an extreme form of elation or irritability that can have profound and damaging effects on a person's life, finances and relationships.

There are many signs and symptoms of mania. These include:

- Increased activity, energy and a feeling of restlessness
- Feeling in an extremely good, high mood
- Extreme irritability
- Unrealistic beliefs in abilities and powers – such as thinking that you're superhuman and can achieve more than mere mortals
- Feeling very easily distracted
- Having poor concentration
- Needing little sleep
- Talking very fast
- Having racing thoughts
- Jumping from one idea to another very quickly
- Going on spending sprees
- Behaving provocatively or aggressively
- Being reckless

- Having an increased sexual drive

- Having poor judgement

- Denying that anything is wrong

Often during an episode of mania, people with schizoaffective disorder may not be aware of the dramatic changes in their behaviour. When the episode is over, they may be shocked, upset and embarrassed by the things that they have done and said.

Mania can be a pleasurable experience – at first. People in the grips of mania tend to feel very enthusiastic and excited, and may come up with a multitude of plans and ideas. However, mania can be very dangerous because it leads to people taking risks that they would not normally take, such as spending too much money, gambling on the stock markets, making unwise investments and pursuing unwise sexual encounters.

Extreme, full blown mania can be a very frightening experience, both for the person experiencing it and for their family and friends. And even when mania seems like a pleasurable experience, it can have devastating effects on a person's life, in areas such as relationships, employment, and finances.

Mania can be classified as being either euphoric or dysphoric. Euphoric mania is the traditional, happy type of mania. Dysphoric mania, on the other hand, makes people very angry, irritable and sometimes aggressive.

What is hypomania?

Hypomania is a mild to moderate form of mania, often described as pleasurable by people with schizoaffective disorder. During an episode of hypomania, people with schizoaffective disorder may experience a feeling of increased optimism and activity, feel more confident and able to get more done. People experiencing a hypomanic episode often enjoy these episodes – but there is always the danger that a hypomanic episode will go on to develop into an episode of full blown mania.

Hypomania is not always a positive experience, however. People who are hypomanic may become increasingly irritable, and feel restless and uptight.

Symptoms of mania in more depth

Increased activity
Increased activity can seem like a positive experience at the start, but it can become increasingly problematic, frenetic and extreme as mania worsens.

Restlessness and agitation
Restlessness can be problematic during manic episodes, causing people to jump from one task to another without completing the first task.

Agitation can make people feel as though they can't sit still.

Becoming more talkative
When people are manic, they talk more and their speech tends to be faster, louder, and more pressured. It can be very difficult to interrupt someone who is manic.

Trying to achieve unrealistic goals
People who are manic tend to focus a lot of their time and increased energy on achieving multiple goals, many of which may be unrealistic. Goals tend to become increasingly numerous and unrealistic as the mania intensifies.

Forgetting to eat

When people are manic, they tend to forget about basic necessities like eating, often because they are in pursuit of unrealistic goals.

Taking risks and acting impulsively

People who are manic have a tendency to start taking risks and/or behaving recklessly. They may drive faster, gamble, or take sexual risks such as sleeping with numerous people. Spending money recklessly is another common problem for people suffering an episode of mania.

Irritability and aggressiveness

People with schizoaffective disorder may experience dysphoric mania and become very irritable and sometimes aggressive. Family and friends may feel as though they are walking on eggshells around the person with dysphoric mania in order not to spark off verbal or physical outbursts.

Heightened senses

People who are experiencing hypomania and mania may feel as though their senses are more acute. Colours may seem brighter and more intense, for example, and sounds, smells and tastes can be magnified.

Increased self-confidence and self-importance

Some people with schizoaffective disorder may experience a sense of power and feel able to achieve anything when they are manic. They may also feel as though the things that they do or who they are has some kind of special importance or significance. Some people may even feel that they are invincible.

Increased sensitivity

Some people, when manic or hypomanic, may be more sensitive to criticism than normal. They can become very defensive and even aggressive if their plans and ideas are challenged.

Racing thoughts

When people are hypomanic, their thoughts seem to be quite quick, but in mania thoughts race, often making people feel as though they can't keep up with their own minds.

Muddled thinking

Thinking can be very clear during episodes of hypomania, but in states of mania, thinking can become quite muddled, as people's attention wanders and they become increasingly distracted. It can be hard to concentrate on just one train of thought. When mania is extreme, people jump from one set of thoughts to another – and there is often no obvious connection between the two.

Having lots of ideas

When people are becoming manic, they tend to have a lot more plans and ideas. Initial, this can make people seem more productive, but as mania increases and becomes more extreme, the ideas tend to become increasingly unrealistic and bizarre.

What is it like to be manic?

Katie[2] shares her story of what it is like to be manic:

Manic Moments

For weeks, the recklessness had been building, the sensation that I was invincible and utterly unstoppable just growing and growing. Too long, I'd been trapped in a dark pit of despair; the freedom from it somehow made the wildness more intense.

---

[2]   Names have been changed to protect identities

For every coherent thought in my mind, there seemed a million more that weren't, crashing together like a pile-up on the M1. The disco-ball rotating above the dance floor was hypnotising me, and my friends had a hidden agenda to get me drunk. Well, why not, it was my eighteenth birthday party after all, and our local club had been hired for the night. It was invitation-only-entry, but as I gazed around the crowded club, I realised *most* of the people were complete strangers. Everything seemed overwhelming, and I wasn't even drunk. Another drink was pressed into my hands; I grinned insincere thanks, waited until Tom walked away, and then poured the contents of the glass into the yucca plant beside me. I didn't need alcohol to make me drunk; I was blissfully intoxicated by the brilliance of life itself, my head bursting with vibrant plans and foolproof schemes. Safely stored in my handbag were the tickets I'd purchased that afternoon for my impromptu trip to Memphis for Elvis week next month. Inside I was fizzling; the beat of the music had melded with the beating of my heart and I felt insuperable.

Amy slid tipsily into the booth, her red hair a frizzy halo around her head. Her glasses were crooked on her face, and she was giggling hopelessly.

'Having fun?' she managed to gasp out, slopping her drink over the table. The party had been her idea. She knew somebody who knew somebody else who managed the club. The drinks weren't free, but they were cheap. I smiled indulgently, every nerve in my body jangling.

The music stopped abruptly. Some fat bloke in a jumpsuit waddled out onto the pathetically small stage. A cheer went up as faces turned expectantly towards me. I stiffened, my facial muscles stubbornly refusing to shape the delighted expression that was expected of me. I stared in horror at the Elvis impersonator as he burst into an awful rendition of *Blue Suede Shoes*. He was a poor imitation of the real thing. My head spun with the volume of the backing track. The same thought kept pounding against the inside of my skull: *He isn't Elvis. He can't be Elvis. **I'm** Elvis. Elvis is dead, and I **am** Elvis.*

I stood up, hopping up onto the booth and vaulting the banister that stood between me and the poky dance floor in front of the stage. 'Elvis' warbled on, oblivious. He finished *Blue Suede Shoes* and launched into *Suspicious Minds*. Or what was supposed to be *Suspicious Minds* – only the melody was distinguishable. He thought he was God's gift, dancing, swinging his hips. The lights spun out of control. Red, green, purple, blue. Red again. Red like the lipstick painted on my lips, a clown smile. Red like blood. He curled his lip, trying to imitate the sneer. A new battery of thought against my skull. *Red like his blood. Red. Red. Red. He's not Elvis. I'm Elvis. He's not **Elvis**.* Others crowded onto the dance floor beside me, too drunk to notice the fury pulsing through my body. Some were even singing along, Tom amongst them. Tom, who should have known better.

'Where's the birthday girl?' 'Elvis' shouted at the end of his song. Tom, laughing, pushed me forward. A really bad move. I was struggling to contain myself, struggling not to erupt, but as the people parted like the parting of the Red Sea, my anger swelled like a relentless wave.

A podgy hand was held out to help me up onto the stage. I stared at it, repulsed by the sight of it. I saw my own hand – my left one, my famous left hand – rising up from my side. And I watched, kind of impassively, as my fingers curled into a fist. My nails were getting too long, I noticed absently. *Must cut them later.*

'Come on up here, Little Lady,' 'Elvis' cajoled.

 The grin slipped from his face in slow motion as we both watched my hand coming up. He reeled back as my fist connected with that sneering mouth, the piggy eyes widening in shock. *Red lights. Red blood.* **He's not Elvis.** I giggled. The collective gasp from behind me was comical. My hand returned obediently to my side as 'Elvis' concertinaed to his knees, and with my other hand, I seized the mic from the stand in front of him. I started laughing helplessly, but managed to splutter into the mic a phrase that had become a trademark for me during two years in the sixth form.

'Ladies and Gentlemen, Elvis has left the building. Thank you and goodnight.'

The place erupted in laughter, though my friends – the dozen or so people there I actually knew – stared at me with half-veiled shock. For some reason, that only made me laugh harder, clutching the mic stand, doubled over in mirth. Behind me, 'Elvis' slowly rose to his feet, staring at me. The lips that he'd tried so hard to curl into the trademark sneer were beginning to swell; blood dribbled lethargically from the split in his bottom lip. The lights spun again. Green. He was an alien. I laughed harder.

'You shouldn't have done that, sweetheart,' he slurred, the words running into one another. He sounded drunk. I was a volcano full of laughter instead of lava. Even as he advanced on me, it didn't occur to me to stop laughing. I *couldn't* stop laughing if I tried. I didn't see the danger. It didn't matter. I was invincible. Superman. No. *Super-Elvis.*

Tom snatched me out of harm's way before 'Elvis' could swing his ape-like arm at me. I struggled to free myself as a fight broke out; I wanted to join in, but Tom held me back, his blue eyes no longer full of laughter.

'Bloody hell,' he swore, dragging me out of the club in the wake of everyone else sober and sensible enough to do the same. 'I know you wanted a birthday to remember, but Christ Almighty! Why did you have to go and hit him?'

'He's not Elvis!' I snapped. '*I'm* Elvis. It was a bloody insult. I had to stop him!'

Tom shook his head, his expression grave. 'Oh God, not *that* again!' he groaned.

I narrowed my eyes at him. 'It's true! It's bloody well true and you know it. And what's more, I'm going to Memphis to prove it!'

Tom didn't believe me. It turns out no one did. They all thought I was a little bit mad. Even the psychiatrist, when I told *him* four years later.

It wasn't *easy* to accept I had an illness, but it helped to put six turbulent years of my life into some kind of perspective.

Chapter Three: Depression and Mixed States

Depression and mixed states are common symptoms in both the bipolar and depressive types of schizoaffective disorder.

What is depression?

Most people will know what it is like to experience periods of sadness or low mood. Depression in schizoaffective disorder is a severe form of low mood and very often leads to suicidal feelings.

Some of the most common signs and symptoms of depression are:

- A lasting depressed or anxious mood
- Feeling hopeless
- Feeling guilty, helpless or worthless
- Losing interest in activities that usually brought feelings of pleasure and/or enjoyment
- Decreased energy
- Feeling slowed down
- Having difficulty concentrating
- Having difficulty remembering things
- Having difficulty making decisions
- Feeling restless or irritable
- Having difficulty sleeping or sleeping too much
- Losing your appetite or eating too much (comfort eating)

- Thinking about death or suicide
- Making suicide attempts

Depression tends to be the most commonly experienced symptom for people with schizoaffective disorder. Depression in schizoaffective disorder is much more than feeling low because of everyday stress and strain, and can be a very distressing experience.

Depression can be experienced in different ways by different people, depending on their combination of symptoms, the severity of the depression and the frequency of depressive episodes. Depression can seem overwhelming and endless, but it is treatable.

What is atypical depression?

People with schizoaffective disorder, like those with bipolar disorder, may experience depression differently from people who have unipolar depression. It is common for people with schizoaffective disorder to experience atypical depression, which means that instead of experiencing insomnia, loss of appetite and being sad and tearful, which are common with typical depression, people feel the need to eat and sleep more and tend to feel very flat and slowed down when they are depressed. Other hallmarks of atypical depression are fatigue and being sensitive to rejection.

Symptoms of depression in more depth

Not being able to feel

A lot of people with schizoaffective disorder experience what they describe as an absence of feeling as part of depressive episodes. This is sometimes also described as feeling flat or empty.

Not caring about anything

People suffering from depression often state that they are unable to care about anything, even things that used to be important to them.

Losing interest and motivation

People with schizoaffective disorder frequently experience a loss of interest in, and motivation to do, things. The things that they used to enjoy don't give them pleasure any more.

Feeling tired and drained of energy

It is common for people experiencing an episode of depression to feel tired all the time. Some people have described this as feeling as though they have just run a marathon and have no energy left.

Feeling worse at particular times of the day

People experiencing an episode of depression may find that they feel worse at particular times of the day. For some people, mornings are worse, whilst for others it is during the evening that they feel worse.

Feeling worthless

People with schizoaffective disorder who are depressed often suffer from feelings of worthlessness. Their self-esteem drops considerably, leaving them lacking in confidence and feeling as though they are useless. Depression can make people forget about their strengths and make them only focus on their weaknesses.

Feeling guilty

Guilt is a very common problem for people experiencing an episode of depression. People tend to feel excessive guilt for minor mistakes and normal human errors.

Becoming more sensitive

When people are depressed they tend to become much more sensitive to both criticism and rejection.

Irritability

It is common for people experiencing depressive or mixed episodes to become much more irritable than usual.

Feeling hopeless and helpless

It is very common for people experiencing depression to feel extremely hopeless about the future and helpless because of feeling unable to change the way they feel.

Feeling worried and anxious

Worry and anxiety are common features of depression. Anxiety can be very disabling for some people. It can be 'global', where everything is a worry, or specific, where anxiety is focused on certain things, for example physical health.

Feeling lethargic

Lethargy, feeling tired, slowed down and unmotivated, is a common symptom for people experiencing episodes of depression. Lethargy can make people talk much slower than usual, use shorter sentences and move around more slowly. In severe forms, lethargy can make it difficult for people to get things done – or even to get out of bed.

Withdrawal and avoidance

It is common for people suffering from depression to withdraw from the things that they used to enjoy doing. They may also start to avoid social situations and turn down invitations from friends.

Thinking negatively

Everyone can think negatively from time to time, but depression has the potential to make people think negatively all the time, or the majority of time. Rumination about past failings is also common in depression.

Sluggish thoughts

One of the hallmarks of depression is the way that people feel as though their head is full of fog. This causes them to have difficulty remembering things or concentrating on things a lot of the time. It can also make decision making and planning very difficult.

What is a mixed state?

A mixed state is where a person with schizoaffective disorder has symptoms of hypomania or mania at the same time as symptoms of depression. This is most common during or following an episode of depression. Manic symptoms in a mixed state tend to include things like irritability, racing thoughts, talkativeness, agitation and being distracted.

Mixed states can be very distressing for people with schizoaffective disorder, because of the combination of symptoms they may experience. Suicidal thoughts are very common, and because of the manic symptoms there is an increased likelihood of a person making a suicide attempt.

What is it like to be depressed?

Jessica[3] explains how she felt when she experienced her first episode of depression:

Dancing With Depression

At sixteen, I suffered my first crippling depression. Oblivious then to the concept of mental illness, I struggled through alone. That I survived has more, I suspect, to do with circumstance than strength of character.

---

[3]   Names have been changed to protect identities

My GCSE results came on three flimsy sheets of paper - one yellow, one pink, one white. An A*, two As, four Bs, and two Ds. Results that anyone should have been proud of. My friend Cassie was ecstatic with her own collection of Ds and Es. But gazing at those tissue-thin pages could only summon feelings of dread. I'd been robbed of the ability to feel anything but bleak, empty misery.

*

Country music blared from the speakers of the community centre as, inside, a motley crew of line-dancing women aged between 16 and 60 danced the night away. Cassie was one of them. *I* should have been one of them. But instead I sat alone on the step outside the French doors, staring at nothing in the half-light of the September night. After line-dancing for over a year, I'd made a sudden and startling discovery: I couldn't do it. Even the most simple grapevine step confounded me. My brain had ground to a halt – along with it any hope of me functioning in the real world.

Despair stalked me like a black dog snapping at my heels. Iron bars of guilt and despondency crashed down around me wherever I went, like a prison wall isolating me from any flickering hope of happiness. Though the late summer sun was glorious, I saw only death and decay – the all-pervading darkness impossible to escape. The music that I had loved made me weep. My failure to function as a human being served up another slab of misery.

Once the thought lodged in my mind, there seemed no escaping it. Death could be my only way out; death was my only viable option. For the first time in weeks, I felt a flicker of excitement. It seemed ironic that only the thought of death could produce such a reaction.

When the music stopped, Cassie came looking for me, her face flushed with exertion. The sight of her happiness only steeled my resolve. Tonight. It had to be tonight, before I lost my nerve.

'Whatcha doin' hiding out here?' Cassie demanded. 'You okay?'

Oh, I'm just fan-bloody-tastic. Isn't it obvious? Can't you see how overjoyed I am with life?

I kept the sarcastic responses to myself. 'I'm fine,' I said, the words dead and meaningless as they crept across my lips. It would have saved time to have them tattooed on my forehead the number of times I'd uttered them lately. People asked, but they didn't care.

'Coming for a drink, then?' Cassie was already heading back inside.

'No.' *You go. Leave me here, and by the time you come back, it'll already be too late.* For the first time in weeks I smiled a genuine smile.

At nine o'clock, it was dark enough for the swings in the playground at the back of the Community Centre to be nothing more than silhouettes in the night. There was a new lightness in my step as I approached them, pulling my belt from my jeans as I walked.

Die, die, die, die. The word rattled, lonely, inside my skull – the only thought my brain now felt worth thinking.

I had no clear concept of how I would do it. Sheer adrenalin made me scale the chains of the first swing and straddle the wooden top-bar. Inside the Centre, the music had started again; for a moment I sat there watching them dancing away, all so innocent of my impending death. I felt a feeling of calm wrap around me like a fleece, though my hands still shook as I threaded my belt through the wide links of the swing chain, manufacturing a pathetic-looking noose. It would have to do. There was no time for anything more elaborate. But I needed to be a contortionist to get my head through. Wrapping my legs tight around the top bar, I hung upside down, white knuckles grasping my makeshift noose as I struggled to slot my head through. It wasn't working. I cried out in desperate frustration as my legs lost their grip on the wood. Hanging by one hand, with leather cutting into my palm, was not how I'd imagined myself being found. In my mind, the image of my dead body swinging in a gentle breeze had been eerily vivid. But I couldn't even kill myself without making a complete cock-up. I dropped back down to the ground, leaving the belt where it was, just to prove to myself that I'd tried. I had the presence of mind to quit line-dancing after that. There seemed little point in torturing myself further. But my dance with death, I didn't forget. It hovered always at the edge of my subconscious, waiting for the next time.

What is it like to experience a mixed state?

Robyn[4] tells the story of one of her more severe mixed episodes:

A Train in My Brain

To die or not to die – now *that* was the question. Shakespeare had got it right, but his version was a little too ambiguous for my liking. My adaptation of the bard's famous line, on the other hand, left little room for uncertainty – and what's more, it summed up my odd relationship with life. To die – for all the times when just being alive took far more effort than it was worth and I went to sleep each night praying not to wake up. Or not to die – for the other times, when being alive was the most amazing feeling on earth and my brain burned with brilliant ideas.

---

[4]   Names have been changed to protect identities

To die, or not to die. To die, or not to die. Again and again, the thought spiralled around my mind like a taunting mantra, pushing me, with every repetition, closer to the edge. I'd grown used to the strange balancing act between mania and depression over the years, but nothing had prepared me for *this:* the strange melding of depression with mania which had left me feeling as though someone had thrust me into the washing machine on a fast spin. It was a lethal combination: the frenzy of mania – the restless energy, the racing thoughts, and the inability to take control of my own mind – coupled with the morbidity of depression. My thoughts were racing, but there was no joy to be found, no bright sparks of revolutionary ideas. No, the primary preoccupation of my spinning brain was death: my own; that, and the crippling fears of persecution that ran amok without the restraint of logic.

My mobile phone began to vibrate, and the young couple opposite me in the pub looked up in surprise as Napoleon's Ghost's 'They're Coming to Take Me Away Ha! Haa!' started to play. There was never, I thought, a more appropriate ring tone than the one I had downloaded the week before. I picked the phone up, glanced at the display, and pressed the 'reject call' button. I didn't want to talk to anyone, for fear that they might, at the very least, try to talk me out of my master-plan.

The plan involved, at its heart, getting very drunk. I knew that the rest of the plan wouldn't be nearly so easy – which was why being drunk was a pre-requisite. My phone rang again and I picked it up, rejected the call, and dropped the phone into the remainder of my pint.

'Try and ring now,' I muttered savagely before draining the glass.

An hour later I left the small, dimly lit pub in the shadow of the Norwich Union building and stumbled, my legs stoutly refusing to obey any command I issued them, towards the pedestrian crossing. The ground rushed up to meet me suddenly, and I lay, dazed, on the pavement for several minutes, whilst people skirted me, shooting me looks of undisguised disgust.

'Part two,' I mumbled, struggling to get back up onto my feet. Clutching the steel railings by the pedestrian crossing, I numbly waited for the green man to urge me to cross. For what seemed like an eternity, the red man glowered mockingly at me, as if daring me to cross the busy intersection without its permission. When finally the green man began to flash, I faltered. Instead of the usual beeping that accompanied the green man, there was a high-pitched voice shrieking '*Bitch! Bitch! Bitch! Bitch! Bitch!*' at me. I lurched across the road, covering my ears with my hands. I bumped into people, but didn't bother to stop to issue an apology. I wasn't sorry – why should I pretend that I was?

The city walls loomed over me as I turned up towards Lendal Bridge. I remembered someone – maybe a history teacher – telling me that there was still a law, left over from medieval times, that said something about it being lawful to shoot a Scotsman from the city walls with a bow and arrow.

'Pity I'm not a Scotsman,' I muttered, 'and Robin Hood's dead.'

There were still a lot of tourists milling about, but I ignored them all as I started walking across Lendal Bridge, running my hand along the white-painted ironwork. When I reached the exact centre of the bridge I stopped, wondering for a moment why it seemed so imperative that I was in the exact centre. I shook my head, unable to remember, and clambered, with uncoordinated limbs, onto the parapet of the bridge, my legs dangling down over the murky water several feet below. I was aware of people staring at me; a few tourists stopped and even dared to take photographs of me. I didn't smile. My head, my whole body in fact, felt heavy with drunkenness, but that – that was all part of the plan. Too drunk to swim, too drunk for any survival mechanisms to try and kick in.

'And now, the end is near, and so I face the final curtain,' I sang, the words slurring into one another. 'The final curtain. All the world's a stage, and I'm a crap actor. Crap. Crap, crap, crap, crap, crap.' The words tumbled from my lips as my befuddled brain formed them. 'Better off dead. The world is better off if I'm dead. Dead as a Dodo. Dead as a *drowned* Dodo.' I stared down into the water, my guts churning with sudden fear. What if I didn't drown? What if someone dragged me out and saved me? What if...

The crossing was bleating again at the end of the street, too loud for my ears. *'Bitch, bitch, bitch, bitch, bitch!'* It was as if the crossing alert had embedded itself in my head. *'Die, die, die, die, die, die, die!'*

'I'm trying,' I moaned. 'I'm trying!'

Drowning wasn't the answer, I suddenly realised. It was too risky. There was too much chance of survival. I swung my legs back over the parapet and fell to the ground in a pathetic heap. Sitting up and hugging my knees, I watched the people passing me by, giving me a wide birth, gazing down in disgust. Their leering faces loomed and receded, and I moaned in horror as I saw the flesh hanging off the bones of their faces. The world was full of dead men walking. Zombies. My fingers scrabbled at the ironwork of the bridge as I dragged myself to my feet and lurched towards the sloping path leading up to the city walls.

The walls formed an arching bridge over the road in two places between Lendal Bridge and Micklegate Bar, with only steel railings preventing some hapless tourist dashing their brains out on the concrete. I found myself smiling, as if the prospect of certain death had tripped some switch in my brain. I was laughing as I straddled the railings on the first road arch.

'Either I fly or I die!' I yelled, flinging my arms out wide and laughing some more, because really, it didn't matter which: fly or die – they rhymed so perfectly, it made the prospect of death seem all the more poetic. My mind seemed to have cleaved in two quite suddenly: half was lamenting the joy of death, whilst the other half seemed certain of invincibility.

'Hey!' There was a shout from the street below, and I waved.

'Hello!' I shouted back, because it seemed like the most normal, polite thing to do.

'Don't jump!' the horrified passer by yelled.

'I was going to fly,' I replied as the man began running up the stone steps up onto the walls.

'Don't jump,' he repeated, gasping as he leaned against the railings close to where I was perched.

I scowled. 'Don't tell me what to do,' I retorted, discarding any thoughts of being polite. 'Who do you think you are, trying to tell me what to do? God? Because I know you're not God. I'm not stupid. God wouldn't tell me not to jump. Do you know why? Because God *wants* me to jump.'

'Please don't jump!' the man begged plaintively.

I tore my fingers through my dark red hair. 'It's nothing to do with you,' I snarled, swinging my other leg over the railings so I was perched on just an inch of metal. The slightest tip in my balance would have me over the edge. It was a soothing prospect. I sighed, breathing in deeply.

'What's your name?' the man asked, speaking slowly as if he was addressing an idiot.

'Jesus,' I muttered, and laughed, because I hadn't meant it like that, like Jesus was my name, but it was as good a name to have anyway. I cocked my head, considering. 'Do you think I'll rise again on the third day?' I asked conversationally, as if there was nothing out of the ordinary about holding a conversation with a complete stranger as I contemplated plunging to my death.

The man didn't answer. He was too busy stabbing his finger at the buttons on his phone, and then frowning as he held it to his ear. 'Police,' he said. 'And Ambulance.'

'Huh?' I stared at him. 'What?'

'There's someone going to jump of the city walls at Station Rise!' the man cried into the phone.

His words bounced meaninglessly around in the inside of my skull and I disregarded them completely. I was finding it hard to hold any thoughts in my head for more than a couple of seconds, and even when I managed it, I was distracted by the way the thoughts seemed to be rocketing around with the same rhythm as a steam train. Clackety-clack, Clackety-clack, Clackety-clack, so the thoughts themselves became meaningless as I listened instead to the rhythm of them.

'Clackety-clack,' I said, smiling to myself as I repeated it over and over.

'Givemeyour-hand, givemeyour-hand,' the man said, and I turned my head to look at him.

'Ohnol-won't, ohnol-won't,' I retorted, tucking my hands under my thighs. I almost lost my balance, but the man grabbed my bag and used it to hold me steady.

The wail of first one, and then another siren split the air and I winced, lifting my hands to cover my ears. Every one of my senses seemed too sharp for comfort; I could smell the man's body odour like it was magnified a dozen times, and the brightness of the sun was making my eyes ache. A police car came to a sudden halt in front of the nearby war memorial, and an ambulance pulled in behind the panda car. I frowned, something finally registering in some distant part of my brain.

'Oh no,' I said, shaking my head. 'No.' There had been an ambulance another time, and a trip to the hospital, and a great escape, though not like Steve McQueen's Great Escape, because the escape had been made on foot. 'No, no, no, no, no, no, no.' Gripping the railings tightly, I clambered back over onto the wall side of the railings and yanked my bag free of the man's grasp. 'No!' I yelled as the police and the paramedics started up the steps onto the walls. I glanced left, then right, unable to decide which way to run. I couldn't think, still, past the train in my brain, and fear was making my heart pound like drums in my ears. As the first police officer reached the top of the steps, I turned and stumbled in the direction of Micklegate Bar. My legs felt like they were made of rubber, wilfully resisting my attempts to properly coordinate them. My shambling gait could hardly be described as running, and my hopes of escape evaporated the moment I encountered shallow steps along the path. I fell headlong; that I thrust out my hands to break my fall was more a coincidence than an actual conscious decision. A pair of hands reached down and helped me to my feet. The policeman regarded me with kind eyes.

'Let's get you to the hospital,' he said, and that was that, the end of my plans. I was admitted to the psychiatric ward that afternoon.

Chapter Four: Psychotic Symptoms

Hallucinations, delusions and thought disorder are common symptoms that people with schizoaffective disorder experience.

What are hallucinations?

Hallucinations are a psychotic symptom of schizoaffective disorder. People experiencing hallucinations may hear, see, smell, taste or feel things that aren't really there, and which other people can't hear, see, smell, taste or feel.

Auditory hallucinations are the most common type of hallucination. They are mostly experienced as voices. To a person with schizoaffective disorder, these voices sound just like people speaking to them, and people with the illness cannot differentiate between what is real – for example a friend speaking to them – and what is a hallucination.

Voices might be heard in the second person – for example someone saying "you stink", "you're ugly", "they hate you". Sometimes voices might command a person to do something – by saying, for example, "jump off the bridge", "take an overdose". People with schizoaffective disorder may also have third person hallucinations, which commonly take the form of two or more voices talking among themselves or commenting on the person's behaviour. Third person hallucinations are common in both schizoaffective disorder and schizophrenia, but are seen less frequently in bipolar disorder.

In most cases the experience of auditory hallucinations in the form of voices is unpleasant. Voices are frequently accusatory, reminding the person of past misdeeds, some imaginary, and some real. However, in a minority of cases, voices can be pleasant or even helpful.

In addition to voices, auditory hallucinations can involve noises, such as buzzing, screeching and ringing. Additionally, people with schizoaffective disorder may think that their own thoughts are being broadcast, or can be heard by other people. They may also think that other people's thoughts are being forced into their own minds, or that their thoughts have been stolen from their heads.

Hallucinations of all five senses may be experienced. In addition to auditory hallucinations, people may have tactile hallucinations – such as feeling as though you are being pushed, touched or held down – visual hallucinations – such as seeing things that aren't there or feeling that colours are brighter than they should be – hallucinations of smell and hallucinations of taste.

Visual hallucinations occur much less frequently than auditory hallucinations, and are more common in conjunction with auditory hallucinations – for example seeing and hearing someone who no one else can see. Hallucinations of smell and taste are more unusual and tend to focus on things tasting or smelling different than usual. This can lead to people with schizoaffective disorder thinking that their family and friends are trying to poison them.

Types and examples of hallucinations

Hallucination Type		Example
Auditory	Voices:	
	Single or multiple	"You smell", "They hate you", "You're ugly

	Arguing, conversing	"He should do it"/ "No, he shouldn't"
		"She's useless"/ "Yes, look at her, how pathetic"
	Commenting	"What's he gone and done that for? He's stupid!"
	Commanding	"Jump off the bridge", "Take an overdose"
	Sounds: • Music • Strange or threatening noises	
Tactile/ Somatic	Hallucinations of touch	Feeling as though you are being held down, feeling as though something is burning you.
Visual	Unusual perceptions of objects or people others can't see	Seeing a little person who talks to you, seeing words flying at you from people's mouths.
Gustatory	Perception of persistent or recurrent bad or unusual tastes	Food tastes different or strange and you think you're being poisoned.
Olfactory	Unusual perceptions of smells that other people don't smell	Smelling burning, smelling gas or other unpleasant smells.

What are delusions?

Delusions are another psychotic symptom of schizoaffective disorder. Delusions are generally described as mistaken interpretations of the things that are going on around people. People with schizoaffective disorder tend to develop fixed, unshakable beliefs based on their psychotic reality, and it is very difficult to try to reason with someone experiencing delusions. This is because to the person experiencing them, the delusions are very real.

Delusional beliefs can be very frightening for the people experiencing them. People may believe that they are being hunted by government agents or that aliens are communicating with them through the radio and television. Sometimes, delusional ideas can be grandiose – for example a person may believe that they are able to control the weather with their thoughts or that they are a member of a royal family.

Delusions are usually formed on the basis of the misinterpretation of sensory experiences. For example, a person may interpret a bit of static on the radio as some kind of message or signal. Random events can be interpreted as relating to the person in some special way.

Delusions can become very complex as they develop further and become more strongly entrenched in a person's mind. For example, a person may start off thinking that they are being watched but go on to believe that they are being controlled or manipulated in some way. They become hyper-vigilant, always on the lookout for "evidence" that may support their beliefs – which they will always find because of their tendency to misinterpret normal everyday events.

Delusions that centre around a person being watched or persecuted are known as paranoid delusions. These are a common type of delusion in schizoaffective disorder. In some cases, paranoid delusions can lead to people in the grip of delusions becoming violent towards the people they think are persecuting them or who are out to harm them. It is rare for someone with schizoaffective disorder to become violent, however; they are more likely to harm themselves than other people in actual fact.

Types and examples of delusions

Delusion Type	Definition	Example
Persecutory delusion	False belief that you or your loved ones are being persecuted, watched or conspired against by others.	Belief that MI5, the CIA/FBI or the police are conspiring to catch you.
Delusions of control	Belief that your thoughts, feelings, or behaviours are being controlled by an external force.	Belief that an alien has taken over your body and is controlling you.
Thought broadcasting	Belief that your thoughts are being broadcast from your mind for others to hear	Belief that your thoughts are being transmitted via the internet against your will
Thought insertion	Belief that another person or object is inserting thoughts into your head	Belief that your wife is inserting thoughts into your mind using the microwave
Thought withdrawal	Belief that thoughts are being removed from your head by	Belief that your work colleagues are extracting

	another person or object	the thoughts from your head using the coffee machine
Delusions of guilt	False belief that you've committed a terrible act or are responsible for something terrible that has happened	Belief that you've killed your husband or wife
Somatic delusions	False belief that your appearance or part of your body is either diseased or has been altered	Belief that your intestines have been replaced by snakes
Grandiose delusions	False belief that you have great power, knowledge or that you're a famous and/ or powerful person	Belief that you are Jesus Christ reincarnated
Delusions of reference	Events, objects or activities of other people are given particular and unusual significance	Believing that the television commentator is mocking you

What is thought disorder?

In severe cases of psychosis, a condition known as thought disorder develops. This means that when a person experiencing thought disorder talks, their sentences don't make sense and they invent new words and phrases. This is sometimes also known as word salad:

Thought Disorder

"Therefore, indecisive masculine tranceptor particles in the wall should internet search alligator defenceless topaz ridiculous water without honestly particulartory tomorrow the diamond with the tranceptoron utilize machine washing erroneous malodour vinigarette till the end defended by entropy through stolen margarine endless tropical malformed misinterpreted hotel room endless…"

What is it like to be psychotic?

David[5] takes us into the world of psychosis:

Distortions of Reality

Psychosis kind of crept up on me. I'd had odd spells of depression, and an episode of what I now know to be hypomania, but I had no idea I was ill. Not until that night at the museum.

There was only me and Max, the night-watchman, still in the building that night. Everyone else had had the good sense to go home, but at nine o'clock I was still pacing the exhibition hall, rehearsing the lecture I was due to give to a bunch of undergraduate students the following day. I am a palaeontologist – which means that I study prehistoric life – and the museum where I was spending a year as palaeontologist in residence was opening a new exhibit of dinosaur bones found in the UK. Some of my own finds, including the bones of a Megalosaurus, were a part of the exhibition, something I should have been proud of, but wasn't, for some unfathomable reason.

---

5   Names have been changed to protect identities

I read through my speech for what felt like the millionth time and then screwed the sheets of paper into a tight ball and hurled it at the nearby life-size robotic model of a Megalosaurus. The creature's eyes flashed red. I blinked, shaking my head. Too many hours spent on my own with nothing but bones for company was starting to mess with my mind.

I turned and gazed down at the Megalosaurus thigh bone, safe in its display case, which had, in effect, brought me to the museum. I should never have accepted the job. I much preferred being out in the field, but the money that had been offered to me was too good to resist.

With a sigh, I squatted down and picked up the crumpled lecture notes, smoothing them out and folding them back into my pocket. I'd had enough for one night. The lecture would have to do as it was. I switched off the lights and used my shoulder to push open the double doors of the exhibition hall. A creepy sensation, the feeling that something was watching me, shuddered suddenly down my spine, making me pause.

"You could have left us where we were."

The voice came out of nowhere, thin and sinister sounding. For a minute, I thought it might be Max playing practical jokes, but that really wasn't his style.

"You *should* have left us where we were."

I backed up against the wall, shaking my head to try to clear the echoing words from my skull. The noise seemed to wrap around me, taking on a mocking tone. As I edged back through the doors, shaking a little, there was a grating noise and the robotic head of the Megalosaurus spun a 180 degree angle, its red eyes flashing menacingly. The huge jaws snapped open, revealing needle-sharp teeth. Its angry roar shook the high windows of the building. I staggered backwards through the doors as the beast lunged forward, clawed hands outstretched. It all seemed real. I had no idea that it was the start of psychosis.

I lurched out of the museum through the nearest emergency exit, leaving the doors banging in the wind, and stumbled away like I was drunk. I started running as soon as I was able to, and I didn't stop until I reached the safety of my apartment.

Triple locking the door, I slid to the floor with my back to the wall, lowering my head into my hands. The brittle voice that had filled the exhibition hall now filled the inside of my skull. When I closed my eyes, I saw the flashing glare and the snapping jaw of the Megalosaurus. A sick feeling settled in my stomach as my mind grappled for a logical explanation for what had happened. Too much coffee. Too many late nights. An overactive imagination.

The brittle voice whispered in my ears: "You should never have found us, never have moved us, never have claimed us. Now you must pay."

I stumbled down the hallway to my bedroom, ramming the pillows from my bed over my head, trying to block out the voice. But nothing could stop it. The whispered threats went on and on. By dawn, I felt exhausted and sick with terror.

"I'll put them back!" I screamed at the ceiling. "I'll put them back, but please, *please* just leave me alone!"

Deep throated laughter echoed around the flat as I scrambled up and snatched up my keys. The laughter followed me all the way back to the museum, ringing in my ears.

The museum's curator gave me an odd look when I dashed into the staff room and rooted throughout the cupboards for the plastic sacks used to transport remains.

Grabbing a couple of sacks, I tore down the corridor to the exhibition hall.

The students had begun to arrive; they were milling around the exhibition hall. A group were gathered around my Megalosaurus bones, discussing how wonderful it must have been to discover an almost complete skeleton. I pushed my way impatiently through them.

"Not wonderful," I snapped, snatching up the thigh bone and shoving it into one of the sacks. Glancing fearfully over my shoulder, I saw the robotic creature's eyes flash red as it glared at me.

"Hey, what are you doing?" one of the students yelled as I grabbed for more of the bones.

"Taking them back," I muttered, wiping sweat from my forehead with the sleeve of my shirt. As the students looked on in horrified fascination, I lifted the sacks, now bulging with bones, and shook them at the Megalosaurus. "See! I'm taking them back. *I'm taking them back!"*

"Uh, are you okay?" A female student approached me tentatively, offering a bone that I'd dropped.

"I should never have taken them," I moaned, snatching the bone. "Weren't mine. Never mine. He wants them back." I gestured wildly at the Megalosaurus, shuddering. "Got to put them back. Then I'll be okay."

Brittle laughter echoed mockingly around the hall. The eyes of the Megalosaurus flashed red again. I winced.

"That's not *all,"* the voice of the bones whispered menacingly in my ear. "You can never undo the damage that you've done."

A terrible screeching sound ripped through the hall. I fell to my knees as the model Pterodactyl came to life and ripped free of the cables suspending the flying beast from the ceiling. It swooped down, aiming its long pointed beak at me.

"I'm sorry! I didn't know!" I screamed, crawling backwards. All around the hall, the exhibits were coming to life, turning their angry stares on me. A pair of Velociraptors hissed furiously, raking the air with their lethal claws. I kept crawling, fast, towards the exit, but the prehistoric beasts just kept on advancing, surrounding me. The bones, spilt from the sacks as I tried to flee, began arranging themselves into a skeleton that rose up and towered menacingly over me.

"Somebody help me!" I screamed, gazing wildly around the room. The students were staring at me like nothing untoward was happening. "Why won't you help me? Why aren't they attacking you?" I rose to my knees, my chest tightening. "You're part of it," I whispered, horrified. "All of you. They won't hurt you because you're part of this! This isn't about the bones. So what is it? What do you want from me?"

I looked frantically from the beasts surrounding me to the students standing watching. It was a conspiracy. If I didn't do something, I was going to die, helpless, whilst the students watched.

Giving the creatures no chance to prepare, I sprang to my feet and darted towards the doors seizing the fire extinguisher from the wall and brandishing it as a weapon. I edged backwards, swinging the fire extinguisher in a wide, protective arc.

Two security guards came at me from behind, startling me. Pinning my arms behind my back, they forced the canister from my grasp. I fought frantically, but they held me fast, dragging me, kicking and screaming, out of the exhibition hall.

As I was manhandled along the corridor, I stared directly into the lens of the nearest CCTV camera. "My name is David Jones and I am being held against my will!" I screamed.

I was taken to the nearest hospital and admitted to a psychiatric ward, where I was subsequently given the diagnosis of schizoaffective disorder. It took me a long time to accept that what I saw and heard at the museum were just symptoms of an illness. I've had other episodes of psychosis since, but thankfully none that were quite so frightening and extreme as my first episode.

Chapter Five: Anxiety

Many people with schizoaffective disorder suffer the symptoms of anxiety as part of their illness.

What is anxiety?

Anxiety is actually a normal human feeling that is linked to the sensation of fear that people experience when they are faced with situations that are either threatening or difficult. Anxiety, therefore, can be a positive experience because it is designed to protect people from danger.

Anxiety is connected to the famous 'fight or flight' response. However, anxiety can also be a very negative experience when it becomes severe or when there is anxiety in response to situations that are neither threatening nor difficult – i.e. when anxiety occurs in response to normal, everyday events.

Anxiety symptoms can be very distressing and disruptive for people with schizoaffective disorder. They can vary from being relatively mild to being quite disabling.

Anxiety can also increase the risk of recurrence of mood episodes in schizoaffective disorder. It is therefore something that often needs treatment with anti-anxiety medications.

Common symptoms of anxiety include:

- Increased heart rate
- Feeling short of breath
- Feeling like you're choking
- Sweating

Schizoaffective Disorder Simplified

- Feeling dizzy
- Feeling cut off from things
- Shaking or trembling
- Difficulty concentrating
- Nausea
- Vomiting
- Diarrhoea
- Pins and needles
- Numbness
- Feeling very cold
- Hot flushes
- Aches and pains
- Indigestion
- Excessive worry
- Intense fear of losing control
- Feelings of dread

Martine Daniel

PART TWO:

TREATMENT OF SCHIZOAFFECTIVE DISORDER

Martine Daniel

Chapter Six: General Introduction to the Treatment of Schizoaffective Disorder

Schizoaffective disorder is usually treated using a combination of medication and psychotherapy. Therapy is often necessary because medication cannot treat the social problems such as isolation, unemployment and poverty that accompany schizoaffective disorder.

What medications are prescribed for schizoaffective disorder?

Because schizoaffective disorder involves symptoms of thought disorder (psychosis), mood disorder and anxiety disorder, treatment with medication usually involves a combination of antipsychotics, mood stabilisers, antidepressants and anti-anxiety medications.

Antipsychotic medications include:

- Amisulpride
- Aripiprazole
- Clozapine
- Olanzapine
- Quetiapine
- Risperidone

See Chapter Seven for more information about antipsychotic medications, including full details of all medications and their side effects.

Mood stabilisers include:
- Lithium
- Valproate

- Carbemazepine
- Lamotrigine

See Chapter Eight for more information about mood stabilisers, including full details of all medications and their side effects.

Antidepressants

There are a large number of antidepressants available which may be used to treat depression in people with schizoaffective disorder. Older, tricyclic antidepressants tend to make depression worse in schizoaffective disorder, but the newer, serotonergic antidepressants have had positive effects in treating depression in schizoaffective disorder.

Some of the most commonly used antidepressants include:

- Fluoxetine
- Paroxetine
- Sertraline
- Citalopram
- Escitalopram
- Venlafaxine
- Bupropion

See Chapter Nine for more information about antidepressants, including full details of the medications and their side effects.

Anti-anxiety medications include:

- Diazepam
- Lorazepam

See Chapter Ten for more information about anti-anxiety medications, including full details of the medications and their side effects.

What kinds of therapy are available for schizoaffective disorder?

Many people with schizoaffective disorder find that psychological therapy, sometimes known as 'talking treatments', are very helpful in reducing distress and the symptoms of the illness when used in conjunction with medications.

Commonly used psychological therapies include:

- Cognitive behavioural therapy (CBT)
- Cognitive analytic therapy (CAT)
- Family therapy
- Creative therapy

See Chapter Eleven for more information about the different types of therapy available for people with schizoaffective disorder.

Chapter Seven: Antipsychotic Medication

What is antipsychotic medication?

Antipsychotic medication is used to treat psychosis, working to eliminate symptoms such as hallucinations, delusions, and thought disorder. Antipsychotics may also be known as neuroleptics or major tranquilisers.

Antipsychotics were first discovered in 1952 by a French psychiatrist called Pierre Deniker. The first antipsychotic was called chlorpromazine (Largactil) and was first used to sedate patients during surgery before it was trialled with people experiencing psychosis.

Antipsychotics are usually classified as either first generation or second generation, known respectively as typical and atypical antipsychotics. First generation antipsychotics are less widely used now as they cause many more side effects than second generation antipsychotics. First generation antipsychotics are generally reserved for people with treatment-resistant psychosis.

First generation antipsychotics tend to cause a wide range of side effects, including extrapyramidal side effects (EPSE) which involves the person making involuntary movements. It was in the late 1970s (in Europe, but not until 1990 in the United States) that the second generation antipsychotics were first used. These drugs were discovered to be less likely to cause EPSE than the first generation antipsychotics, which is the main reason why second generation antipsychotics are more frequently prescribed today. By 1997, more than half of the people in the United States taking antipsychotic medication were taking second generation antipsychotics.

How do antipsychotics work?

Antipsychotics work by blocking or influencing the action of specific chemicals in the brain known as neurotransmitters. One of these neurotransmitters is called dopamine, which is involved in psychotic symptoms. Antipsychotics reduce the action of dopamine in the brain, therefore helping to reduce or eliminate psychotic symptoms. They reduce the action of dopamine by attaching themselves to the end of the cells that use dopamine as a neurotransmitter, so blocking their action.

How effective are antipsychotics?

Antipsychotics are effective in up to 80% of people suffering from the symptoms of psychosis. However, it may take months or even years to find the right antipsychotic for a person because different people respond to different medication in different ways.

What about the mood stabilising effects of antipsychotics?

Some of the second generation, atypical, antipsychotics have been shown to have a mood stabilising effect. Atypical antipsychotics tend to be quite effective in reducing mania and hypomania. Some antipsychotics also work to treat depression, such as olanzapine, quetiapine and aripiprazole. Olanzapine, quetiapine and aripiprazole can also help to prevent further mood episodes.

What side effects can antipsychotics cause?

All antipsychotic medication has the potential to cause a wide range of side effects, as patient information leaflets accompanying the various medications all state. It is important to remember that different people react differently to different medications and some people are more prone to experiencing side effects than others.

Generally, however, antipsychotic medication is considered to be quite safe to use.

The following are some of the common side effects associated with antipsychotics:

Extrapyramidal side effects (EPSE)

Extrapyramidal side effects tend to occur because antipsychotics block the dopamine using brain cells in the nigro-striatal system in the brain. Up to 80% of people on first generation antipsychotics are affected by EPSE, although some people may experience EPSE on second generation antipsychotics as well.

Most extrapyramidal side effects are reversible, although in some rare cases they may become permanent. Reversible EPSEs include:

- Dystonic reaction – a cramp-like muscle spasm and stiffness

- Dystonia – a sustained cramp-like abnormality of posture that is associated with muscle stiffness

- Akathiia – a sense of restlessness in muscles combined with an inability to sit still

- Parkinsonian symptoms – including rhythmic tremor and immobility of the muscles.

These side effects can be treated with drugs such as procyclidine or propanolol – but it is often better to switch to a different antipsychotic.

Tardive dyskinesia is a rare EPSE, mainly seen in conjunction with first generation antipsychotics. It involves a permanent tremor or a dystonic movement disorder.

Anti-cholinergic (muscarinic) side effects

These side effects occur because of the way antipsychotics attach themselves to cell receptors in the body that are called muscarinic receptors. These side effects include:

- Rapid heart rate
- Dry mouth
- Inability or difficulty in urinating
- Constipation
- Blurred vision

These types of side effects usually wear off after a while and are rarely serious enough to warrant stopping taking the medication.

Anti-adrenergic side effects

This type of side effect generally includes postural hypotension (a sudden drop in blood pressure when standing up) and an inability to ejaculate. These side effects usually wear off after a while and are not serious enough to warrant stopping taking the medication.

Raised prolactin

Prolactin is a hormone, found in both men and women, which increases production during pregnancy and facilitates breast milk production. Rises in prolactin levels are associated with reductions in libido and fertility.

Most of the first generation antipsychotics and some of the second generation antipsychotics cause rises in prolactin to ten times or more the normal levels. This causes women's periods to stop and men to experience erectile failure. Both men and women can experience breast enlargement and milk production. High levels of prolactin are also associated with osteoporosis (reduced bone density) in both men and women.

Weight gain

Antipsychotic medication can cause varying levels of weight gain because it causes the person to feel hungry and therefore eat more. Some people who are strong willed are able to avoid weight gain, but for most people weight gain is a significant problem with most antipsychotic medications.

What antipsychotic medications are available?

First generation anti-psychotics (typical antipsychotics)

First generation antipsychotics are much less widely used, but, in some treatment resistant cases of psychosis, may be necessary.

First generation antipsychotics include:

Group one phenothiazines

These are more sedative and carry a moderate risk of EPSEs and anti-muscarinic side effects.

- Chlorpromazine (Largactil)
- Levomepromazine (Nozinan)
- Promazine (Promazine)

Group two phenothiazines

These are only moderately sedative, and are less likely to causes EPSE, but cause marked anti-muscarinic side effects.

- Pericyazine (Neulactil)
- Pipothiazine (Piportil)

Group three phenothiazines and other first generation antipsychotics

These are more likely to cause EPSEs, but have fewer sedative effects and fewer anti-muscarinic effects.

- Fluphenazine (Modecate)

- Perphenzaine (Fentazin)

- Prochlorperazine (Stemetil)

- Benperidol (Benquil)

- Haloperidol (Haldol)

- Pimozide (Orap)

- Flupentixol (Fluanxol)

- Sulpiride (Dolmatil)

Second generation antipsychotics (atypical antipsychotics)

NICE (the National Institute for Clinical Excellence) guidelines recommend that atypical, second generation antipsychotics should be the first choice when people are experiencing their first episode of psychosis.

The second generation antipsychotics currently available are:

Amisulpride (Solion)

This antipsychotic tends to cause raised prolactin levels and has, in some cases, caused EPSEs. It may also cause insomnia. On the plus side, it has less of a chance of causing weight gain.

Aripiprazole (Abilify)

This is the most recent antipsychotic. Its most common side effects are nausea, vomiting, anxiety and insomnia. It has on occasion caused akathisia. On the plus side, it does not cause raised prolactin levels or cause weight gain. Aripiprazole may be used to stabilise moods as well as alleviate psychotic symptoms.

Clozapine (Clozaril, Denzapine, Zaponex)

This is a special kind of antipsychotic, usually reserved for people with treatment-resistant psychosis or who can't tolerate other antipsychotic medications. It was the first atypical antipsychotic, introduced into Europe in the late 1970s and into the United States in 1990.

Regular blood tests must be done with this medication due to its potential to cause a decrease in white blood cells in some people. Sedation is a major problem with this antipsychotic, as is weight gain. On the plus side, it is not likely to cause a rise in prolactin levels or cause EPSEs

Olanzapine (Zyprexa)

The most common side effects with olanzapine are sedation, weight gain, some anti-muscarinic side effects such as constipation, and a transient rise in prolactin levels. It may also cause EPSEs in some people. Olanzapine is also licensed as a mood stabiliser as well as being used to alleviate psychotic symptoms.

Quetiapine (Seroquel)

The most common side effects with this antipsychotic are postural hypotension, sedation, dry mouth, weight gain, constipation and heart conduction problems. The good news is that there is very little risk of EPSEs with quetiapine and it doesn't cause raised prolactin levels. Quetiapine is also used to stabilise moods as well as alleviate the symptoms of psychosis.

Risperidone (Risperdal)

The most common side effects with risperidone are postural hypotension, raised prolactin levels, insomnia, agitation, headaches and sexual dysfunction. It may also cause EPSEs in some people, and has been associated with weight gain.

Chapter Eight: Mood Stabilising Medication

What are mood stabilisers?

Mood stabilisers, as the name suggests, work to control the symptoms of hypomania, mania, depression and mixed states in schizoaffective disorder. Mood stabilisers act on the active episodes as well as helping to prevent or reduce the number of subsequent episodes of illness.

Medications can only be described as mood stabilising if they don't cause rapid cycling (where there are rapid switches between mania and depression) or bring about the opposite mood episode. For example, medication that treats episodes of depression should not increase the risk of a manic episode.

Mood stabilisers have a regulatory effect on moods – but they do not take away the cause of the mood disorder, and therefore it is important not to stop taking mood stabilisers suddenly because this increases the risk of relapse.

Lithium was the first medication to be described as a mood stabiliser. Other mood stabilisers such as valporate and carbamazepine are actually anti-convulsants – drugs used to treat epileptic fits – that were discovered to also have mood stabilising effects.

How do mood stabilisers work?

It is not yet fully understood how mood stabilisers work. They do have effects on what is known as cell signalling, whereby they alter the passage of information between nerve cells. Different mood stabilisers appear to work in different ways, too. Lithium affects the neurotransmitter serotonin, whilst valporate alters the neurotransmitter GABA and lamotrigine has an effect on the neurotransmitter glutamate. Some mood stabilisers have been found to have effects on the cell membranes, affecting the sodium and calcium channels of the membranes.

Lithium is thought to affect the so-called body clock which serves to regulate biological rhythms. Additionally, most mood stabilisers have the effect of increasing nerve growth factors which help to promote the survival and growth of neurons.

How effective are mood stabilisers?

There has only been limited research done on the efficiency of mood stabilisers and much of the research that has been done centres on lithium. 65% of people respond (i.e. experience a reduction in symptoms of 50%) to lithium. Lithium is, however, more effective in reducing symptoms of mania than it is in reducing the symptoms of depression.

People taking valporate, an anti-convulsant mood stabiliser, respond to the medication between 48% and 80% of the time in episodes of acute mania, but little effect is seen in episodes of depression.

What side effects do mood stabilisers have?

Because the different mood stabilisers work in different ways, there are few side effects that are common to all mood stabilisers. See below for details of the side effects produced by the individual medications.

What mood stabilisers are currently available?

Lithium

Lithium is the oldest and best established treatment for the symptoms of mood disorders. It is usually given in the form of lithium carbonate, which is a naturally occurring salt. It was originally used to treat acute episodes of mania but has also been shown to be effective in preventing the recurrence of mood episodes. Lithium may also be useful in treating and preventing episodes of depression.

Warnings about lithium

Lithium is very effective in treating episodes of mood disorder in schizoaffective disorder but it should not be stopped suddenly, as sudden cessation if the drug can cause dramatic new episodes that are more extreme than moral mood episodes.

Most people are able to take lithium, but it is important for blood tests to be done before starting lithium treatment, primarily to check kidney function as lithium is excreted through the kidneys.

It is essential for lithium levels to be monitored with regular blood tests. This is because if the level is too low, the drug will not be effective, and if it is too high, serious side effects can develop.

Lithium levels can become too high if the dose is too high or if the person taking the drug becomes dehydrated, which can happen with vomiting, diarrhoea and heavy sweating. Some medications, such as diuretics, anti-inflammatory drugs and blood pressure medications can also increase lithium levels.

Lithium toxicity

If lithium levels become too high, people can experience something called lithium toxicity. The signs of lithium toxicity are:

- Persistent diarrhoea
- Vomiting or severe nausea
- Trembling

- Weakness or twitching of hands or legs
- Blurred vision
- Slurred speech
- Unsteady gait
- Dizziness
- Swelling of feet and lower legs

If people experience any of these symptoms, they should contact their doctor immediately, as lithium toxicity can be dangerous.

Side effects of lithium

Most of the side effects seen in lithium are connected to blood levels. The majority of people don't get side effects but some people may experience side effects when they first start lithium therapy or when their dosage is increased. The following side effects may be experienced:

- Increased thirst
- Increased urination
- Nausea
- Mild stomach cramps
- Mental dulling
- Fine tremor of the hands
- Mild sleepiness
- Decreased sexual ability
- Slight dizziness
- Weight gain
- Dry mouth
- Worsening of acne or psoriasis

Most side effects will disappear after a few weeks of treatment. The side effects that may persist after this time are increased thirst, frequent urination, weight gain and fine tremor of the hands.

Pregnancy and breast feeding concerns

The use of lithium during the first three months of pregnancy has been linked to an increased risk of heart abnormalities in babies.

Lithium is excreted in breast milk, so mothers taking lithium should not breastfeed.

Valporate

Valporate is a drug that was initially used only as an anti-convulsant in the treatment of epilepsy. Its mood stabilising properties were then noticed in people who were taking it.

Valporate, like lithium, is effective in the treatment of mania and hypomania and as an agent to prevent relapse. It has some efficiency in depression, although this is slight.

Valporate may work more quickly than lithium in manic states, but as a general rule it may take several months before the full effects of valporate are achieved.

Blood tests are also necessary with valporate, although these are less important than with lithium.

Side effects of valporate

Not everyone taking valporate will experience all the possible side effects but most people will experience one or two side effects. Weight gain, for example, is relatively common. Other common side effects include:

- Nausea
- Sedation
- Being unsteady on the feet

- Indigestion

Less common side effects include:

- Swelling
- Visual changes
- Hair loss or thinning

Pregnancy and breast feeding concerns

Valporate has been found to cause congenital abnormalities in babies whose mothers took the drug during the first few months of pregnancy. The most significant abnormality with valporate is spina bifida. Because of this, it is not advisable for someone to take valporate if they are planning on getting pregnant.

Carbamazepine

Carbamazepine, like valporate, was initially used as an anti-convulsant to treat epilepsy. In schizoaffective disorder, carbamazepine can be useful in reducing the effects of mania, hypomania and mixed episodes, and in preventing future episodes. It is particularly effective for people who have not responded to lithium.

Like other mood stabilisers, carbamazepine takes several months to achieve its full efficiency in treating the mood disorder aspect of schizoaffective disorder.

Warnings about carbamazepine

In rare cases, carbamazepine can lead to a serious drop in the white blood cell count and so the blood count needs to be monitored regularly whilst people are taking the medication. Signs of lowered white blood count include:

- Fever
- Infection

- Sore throat

- Sores in the mouth

- Easily bruising or bleeding

People taking carbamazepine should inform their doctor immediately if they experience the above symptoms.

Carbamazepine can also have effects on the liver, sodium levels and thyroid.

Side effects of carbamazepine

As with all medications, side effects are possible with carbamazepine. The most common side effects are nausea, vomiting and diarrhoea, but these effects usually improve once the person has been taking carbamazepine for a few weeks. Mild memory impairment can also occur quite frequently in the first few weeks of treatment, but generally improves with time.

Other side effects include:

- Blurred or double vision
- Drowsiness
- Unsteadiness
- Unusual tiredness

About 10-15% of people taking carbamazepine have reported skin rashes as a side effect of the medication. This should be reported to a doctor immediately as it can be a sign of a more serious skin condition that usually requires treatment.

Lamotrigine

Lamotrigine is another anti-convulsant medication that was found to have mood stabilising effects. It is most effective in the treatment of depression in schizoaffective disorder.

Unlike other mood stabilisers, it is less effective in treating mania. As an ongoing treatment, lamotrigine is useful in preventing further episodes of depression, mania and hypomania.

Lamotrigine has been found to be effective in treating people with schizoaffective disorder who haven't responded to other mood stabilising medications.

Warnings about lamotrigine

The dosage of lamotrigine must be increased slowly as the mediation can cause a potentially serious rash. The rash is seen in 6-10% of people within the first 2-8 weeks of treatment.

Side effects of lamotrigine

Side effects with lamotrigine tend to be mild and transient and include:

- Problems with physical coordination

- Dizziness

- Drowsiness

- Nausea

- Vomiting

- Headaches

Chapter Nine: Antidepressant Medications

What are antidepressants?

Antidepressants, as their name suggests, are medications that can be used to treat episodes of depression in schizoaffective disorder. Antidepressants can be highly effective in alleviating the symptoms of depression, but should be used with caution in people with mood disorders because of their tendency to cause switches to hypomania, mania and mixed episodes. Antidepressants are usually prescribed in conjunction with mood stabilisers or antipsychotics in schizoaffective disorder.

There are several different types of antidepressants. The most commonly used are called selective serotonin reuptake inhibitors (SSRIs). Other types of antidepressants include dual reuptake inhibitors, monoamine oxidase inhibitors (MAOIs) and tricyclic antidepressants.

SSRIs are the type of antidepressants that are most commonly prescribed because they have fewer side effects and have a lesser chance of causing mania, hypomania and mixed episodes than other, older, antidepressants. SSRIs may also help to reduce the symptoms of anxiety that are common with schizoaffective disorder.

Dual reuptake inhibitors have an effect on serotonin and noradrenalin. These antidepressants also have fewer side effects than older antidepressants, but have a higher risk of triggering hypomania and mania than SSRIs.

MAOIs are prescribed mainly when SSRIs and dual reuptake inhibitors have not been effective. They have to be used with caution because they can cause a dangerous rise in blood pressure. People taking MAOIs have to be on a special diet that eliminates cheese and certain other foods which can increase the risk of raised blood pressure.

Tricyclic antidepressants are an older type of antidepressant that have a far greater side effect profile and cause switches to mania and hypomania. These antidepressants have a tendency to worsen symptoms in people with schizoaffective disorder, and should be avoided.

How do antidepressants work?

Researchers actually know very little about how antidepressants work, but it is thought that because depression may be caused by low levels of serotonin, antidepressants help to increase the levels of serotonin in the brain.

How effective are antidepressants?

Although many people with severe depression have been helped by antidepressant medication it doesn't work for everyone. A major study in 2006 revealed that less than 50% of people treated with two different antidepressants became free of symptoms. Even people who do respond to antidepressants later relapse back into depression even if they continue to take their medication as prescribed.

The benefits of antidepressants have been exaggerated by some drug companies, particularly with regard to mild to moderate depression, when antidepressants are only slightly more effective than placebos.

What side effects do antidepressants have?

Side effects vary according to the type of antidepressants being taken. The following are some common side effects categorised by the type of antidepressant.

SSRIs

SSRIs act on serotonin, which is thought to be a contributing factor to depression. Serotonin, however, also plays a role in digestion, sleep, pain, mental clarity and other bodily functions, so SSRI antidepressants tend to cause a wide range of side effects.

Common side effects in SSRIs include:

- Sexual problems
- Insomnia
- Weight gain or loss
- Diarrhoea
- Drowsiness
- Anxiety
- Tremors
- Constipation
- Sleep difficulties
- Restlessness
- Sweating
- Headaches
- Nausea
- Dizziness
- Dry mouth
- Sleepiness

Additionally, in people over 65, SSRIs may increase the risk of falls, fractures and bone density loss.

SSRIs can cause serious withdrawal symptoms if people stop taking them suddenly.

Dual reuptake inhibitors and other 'atypical' antidepressants

The side effects of these newer types of antidepressants, which include bupropion and venlafaxine, vary according to the drug being taken, but some common side effects include:

- Nausea
- Fatigue
- Weight gain
- Sleepiness
- Nervousness
- Dry mouth
- Blurred vision

What about the risk of suicide with antidepressants?

There is a danger that for some people antidepressant medication will cause an increase in depressive symptoms and therefore increase the risk of suicide. This is particularly true of children and young adults, but anyone taking antidepressant medication should be closely monitored for signs that their condition is worsening. The suicide risk is greatest during the first two months of antidepressant treatment.

The warning signs to look out for are:

- Suicidal thoughts or attempts
- New or worse depression
- New or worse anxiety
- New or worse irritability
- Feeling agitated or restless

- Difficulty sleeping
- Aggression and anger
- Acting on dangerous impulses
- Extreme hyperactivity
- Other unusual changes in behaviour

Why should antidepressants not be stopped suddenly?

Stopping antidepressant medication is not as simple as just stopping taking them when you feel better. Many people have withdrawal symptoms when they stop antidepressants, so it is essential not to stop taking them suddenly but instead taper them off slowly.

Antidepressant discontinuation syndrome consists of symptoms such as:

- Anxiety and agitation
- Depression and mood swings
- Flu-like symptoms
- Irritability and aggression
- Insomnia or nightmares
- Nausea and vomiting
- Dizziness and loss of coordination
- Stomach cramping and pain
- Electric shock sensations
- Tremor, muscle spasms

When depression is a withdrawal symptom, it is often worse than the original depression, but unfortunately many people mistake the withdrawal symptom for a return of their original depression and resume taking the medication.

In order to avoid antidepressant withdrawal symptoms it is important to taper the dose, allowing at least 1-2 weeks between each dosage reduction. The tapering process may therefore take several months.

What antidepressants are available?

SSRIs

Citalopram (Celexa)

Citalopram causes relatively mild withdrawal symptoms and doesn't usually interact with other medications.

Side effects include:

- Diarrhoea
- Constipation
- Sexual dysfunction
- Anxiety
- Insomnia
- Headache
- Tremor
- Dizziness
- Drowsiness
- Dry mouth
- Suicidal thoughts

Escitalopram (Lexapro)

Escitalopram is chemically very similar to citalopram but is more effective and has a faster onset than citalopram. It is a highly selective SSRI.

Side effects include:

- Diarrhoea
- Constipation
- Sexual dysfunction
- Anxiety
- Insomnia
- Headache
- Tremor
- Dizziness
- Drowsiness
- Dry mouth
- Suicidal thoughts

Fluoxetine (Prozac)

Fluoxetine has a slower onset of antidepressant effect than most antidepressants, and is more likely to cause agitation, nervousness and anxiety. On the plus side, it's less likely to cause discontinuation symptoms.

Side effects include:

- Headache
- Nervousness
- Insomnia
- Anxiety

- Nausea
- Diarrhoea
- Sexual dysfunction
- Suicidal thoughts

Paroxetine (Paxil)

Paroxetine is particularly effective in treating the anxiety that is often associated with depression. However, paroxetine causes more sexual dysfunction and weight gain and causes severe withdrawal symptoms.

Side effects include:

- Nausea
- Diarrhoea
- Sweating
- Drowsiness
- Dizziness
- Sexual dysfunction
- Nervousness
- Anxiety
- Suicidal thoughts

Sertraline (Zoloft)

Sertraline has a tendency to cause diarrhoea but has less chance of causing weight gain and doesn't interact with other drugs. Sertraline may be useful in older adults because it does not have anticholinergic side effects.

Side effects include:

- Nausea

- Vomiting
- Diarrhoea
- Insomnia
- Sleepiness
- Anxiety
- Sexual dysfunction
- Suicidal thoughts
- Rash

Dual reuptake inhibitors and other atypical antidepressants

Venlafaxine (Effexor)

Venlafaxine tends to alleviate symptoms of depression better than other antidepressants. In terms of side effects, though, venlafaxine is inferior to SSRIs, being associated with a higher rate of nausea and vomiting. In addition, the drug also has a high incidence of discontinuation symptoms.

Side effects include:

- Nausea
- Vomiting
- Restlessness
- Insomnia
- Weakness
- Blurred vision
- Drowsiness
- Dizziness

- Sexual dysfunction
- Hypertension
- Palpitations
- Suicidal thoughts or attempts

Bupropion (Wellbutrin SR, Wellbutrin XL)

Bupropion is a unique drug with a chemical structure that is unrelated to other antidepressants. This antidepressant rarely causes sexual dysfunction and in the long term can result in a small weight loss.

Side effects include:

- Insomnia
- Poor concentration
- Headache
- Dizziness
- Nausea
- Vomiting
- Rash
- Fever
- Jaundice
- Confusion
- Anxiety
- Palpitations
- Seizures

Chapter Ten: Anti-anxiety Medications

What are anti-anxiety medications?

Anti-anxiety medications consist of benzodiazepines and so-called Z-drugs. They are used to treat anxiety and sleeping problems associated with depression in schizoaffective disorder. Z drugs are so called because the medications in this class all begin with the letter Z.

Anti-anxiety medications are highly addictive medications and should really only be used for short periods of time.

How do anti-anxiety medications work?

Anti-anxiety medications work by affecting the way that specific brain chemicals – neurotransmitters – transmit messages to certain brain cells. They thus have the effect of decreasing the 'excitability' of some brain cells, which has a calming effect on brain functions.

How effective are anti-anxiety medications?

Benzodiazepines and Z drugs seem to be very effective in alleviating the symptoms of anxiety that people with schizoaffective disorder may experience, particularly when the person first starts taking them. Short courses of anti-anxiety medications are usually most effective as these drugs seem to lose some of their efficiency the longer period of time they are taken for. These medications, therefore, are not recommended for long-term anxiety problems.

Why shouldn't anti-anxiety medications be taken for long periods of time?

Anti-anxiety medications should only be taken for short periods of time. This is because after 2-4 weeks of treatment with anti-anxiety medications, certain problems can arise.

Tolerance

After the first few weeks of treatment with benzodiazepines and Z drugs, the body and the brain both become used to the drug and therefore the medication starts to lose its effect. The initial dose becomes ineffective and the person needs increasingly higher doses of medication in order to get relief from their symptoms. This effect is called tolerance.

Dependence (addiction)

If people take anti-anxiety medications for more than four weeks at a time, there is a good chance that they will become dependent on the drug. This means that the person will get withdrawal symptoms if they try to stop the medication suddenly. It feels as though they need the medication in order to feel 'normal'.

Withdrawal symptoms can include:

- Psychological symptoms
    - Anxiety
    - Panic attacks
    - Odd sensations
    - Feelings of unreality
    - Feeling as though you are outside of your body
- Physical symptoms

- o Sweating
- o Insomnia
- o Headache
- o Tremor
- o Feeling sick
- o Palpitations
- o Muscle spasms
- o Being over sensitive to light, sound and touch

Withdrawal symptoms may last for up to six weeks – occasionally longer. They are usually worse for the first couple of weeks after stopping taking anti-anxiety medication.

What side effects do anti-anxiety medications have?

Anti-anxiety medications work by reducing brain activity, and whilst this helps to alleviate anxiety symptoms, it also causes side effects.

The higher the dose, the more pronounced the side effects become. Some people, however, experience side effects even on low doses of these medications.

Common side effects with anti-anxiety medications include:

- Drowsiness
- Lack of energy
- Clumsiness
- Slow reflexes
- Slurred speech
- Confusion and disorientation

- Depression
- Dizziness
- Light-headedness
- Impaired thinking and judgement
- Memory loss
- Forgetfulness
- Nausea
- Blurred or double vision

What anti-anxiety medications are currently available?

Benzodiazepines
- Diazepam (Valium)
- Oxazepam
- Temazepam
- Lorazepam (Ativan)
- Nitrazepam
- Flurazepam
- Chloroliazeproxide (Librium)
- Lorazolam
- Lormetazepam
- Alprazolam (Xanax)
- Clobazam
- Donazepam

Z drugs
- Zaleplon

- Zolpidem
- Zopiclone

Chapter Eleven: Psychological Therapies for Schizoaffective Disorder

What are psychological therapies?

Psychological therapies are sometime referred to as talking treatments. They can be extremely beneficial for people suffering with the symptoms of schizoaffective disorder. Psychological therapies can help to reduce distress and symptoms by helping people to find new ways of thinking and allowing them to talk about their problems.

Psychological therapies were originally thought to be mainly beneficial for people with mild to moderate problems such as unipolar depression and anxiety, but research has found that psychological therapies are also effective in people with more serious illnesses like schizoaffective disorder.

Psychological therapies involve people talking through their problems with trained professionals, with the aim of improving their quality of life. Psychological therapies can therefore help people to manage the symptoms of their illness and help to tackle patterns of negative thinking that are common during episodes of depression in schizoaffective disorder.

There are a number of different psychological therapies suitable for people with schizoaffective disorder. These include:

- Cognitive behavioural therapy (CBT)

- Cognitive analytic therapy (CAT)

- Family therapy (sometimes known as family intervention)

- Creative therapy

Are psychological therapies readily available?

In the United Kingdom, psychological therapies are available both privately and on the NHS.

The benefits of private therapy are an increased choice of treatment types and therapies, faster access to therapy and the ability to change therapists if for some reason the person is dissatisfied with their therapist. However, the cost of private treatment is a massive drawback – it can cost as much as £50 per session, sometimes more – although some therapists offer reduction in rates for people on low incomes.

Therapy is available on the NHS and people typically access this via referrals made by their GP or other mental health professionals. There are a range of treatments available on the NHS but the main drawback to therapy on the NHS is the length of time people have to wait after the initial referral has been made. The wait can be anything from six months to two years.

What is cognitive behavioural therapy?

Cognitive behavioural therapy is a type of psychotherapy that aims to help people to overcome their emotional problems, such as those experienced as part of schizoaffective disorder. One of the central concepts of CBT is that people 'feel how they think'. This means that people are better able to cope with life if they are able to counteract some of their negative thinking patterns. This is particularly true of depressive symptoms in schizoaffective disorder. In fact, cognitive behavioural therapy was originally developed as a treatment for depression.

Recently, however, CBT has been developed for people experiencing the hallucinations and delusions of psychosis.

In CBT for psychosis, people with schizoaffective disorder are taught to take responsibility for, and control of, their psychotic experiences. The goal of therapy is to reduce the distress associated with delusional beliefs and hallucinations, and to learn to contradict beliefs by weighing evidence, as well as evaluating negative beliefs.

CBT looks at the links between thoughts, feelings and behaviours. Feelings result from the way that people interpret and make sense of the world, but in psychosis this process doesn't work properly, leading to hallucinations and delusions. In depression, negative thoughts result in people feeling sad, hopeless and depressed.

In CBT, the acronym "ABC" is often used to look at the process:

- A = Activating event
- B = Belief about the event
- C = Consequence – feelings and behaviours

Being able to challenge or think differently about thoughts, beliefs and hallucinations means that a person with schizoaffective disorder is less likely to feel distressed.

Cognitive behavioural therapy typically requires between 10 and 15 sessions to be effective.

What is cognitive analytic therapy?

Cognitive analytic therapy is a type of therapy that looks at what has hindered changes in the past so that the person can move forward in the present. CAT makes answering questions like "why do I always end up feeling like this?" easier.

Cognitive analytic therapy involves discovering what has caused problems in the past and why the person has developed ineffective coping mechanisms. CAT also helps people to understand how their coping mechanisms could be making their problems worse. The therapy then helps the person to adapt their coping mechanisms to make them more effective.

Diagrams and written outlines are often used in CAT to formulate the person's problems and to identify pathways to change.

An average number of 16 sessions of cognitive analytic therapy are usually offered to people wanting to access this type of therapy.

What is family therapy?

Family therapy, sometimes called family intervention, is a type of therapy that was originally designed to help families deal with a member of the family who was suffering from some kind of addiction or other self-destructive behaviour. However, the family intervention programme has been adapted to help families caring for people with schizoaffective disorder and other related mental illnesses such as bipolar disorder and schizophrenia.

Family intervention helps people with schizoaffective disorder and their families to come to terms with the diagnosis, learn how to manage stress, learn how to solve problems that may arise, and help them to communicate more effectively.

Family interventions have been shown to be effective in delaying and sometimes preventing relapse in people with schizoaffective disorder.

What are creative therapies?

Creative therapies are a type of therapy which uses art and drama in order to increase a person's self-awareness, help them to develop social skills, reduce their anxiety and help to increase their self-esteem.

Art therapy is a creative therapy in which people are encouraged to express their emotions and explore their problems using art materials such as paint, pencils, pastels, crayons etc. Art therapy can be very useful for people who have trouble expressing themselves in words.

Drama therapy is a creative therapy that uses theatrical techniques, such as role play and storytelling to assist in expression and insight.

Are there any risks with psychological therapies?

There is always the risk with psychological therapies that focusing on problems can make a person feel worse. There is an additional risk that people may come to feel dependent on their therapist. They may also experience very strong feelings of attachment to their therapist.

However, these risks are slight when compared to the potential benefits of psychological therapies.

PART THREE:
LIVING WITH SCHIZOAFFECTIVE DISORDER

Martine Daniel

Chapter Twelve: Living Well with Schizoaffective Disorder

When people are first diagnosed with schizoaffective disorder, it can often feel as though the illness controls them and this can lead to feelings of helplessness. Fortunately, there are things that people can do to take back a bit of control and help themselves.

Developing good habits

Developing good habits such as regular exercise, managing stress and eating a healthy diet can be extremely beneficial for people with schizoaffective disorder.

Exercise

When people exercise, their bodies release natural body chemicals called endorphins which can help to reduce stress. Exercise has also been found to help reduce depression and anxiety. It can also help people with schizoaffective disorder to cope with the psychotic symptoms of their illness.

In addition, exercise may help to stimulate new brain cell growth and can help to combat some of the side effects of antipsychotics, particularly the weight gain that is seen with most antipsychotics.

Experts recommend that people exercise regularly to get the full benefit. Regular exercise is classified as at least 20 minutes, three times a week, of exercise that raises the heart rate, such as brisk walking, jogging, cycling, swimming and aerobics.

Managing stress

Stress is a common part of everybody's lives and a healthy amount of stress can help to motivate and challenge people in a positive way. Too much stress, however, can trigger episodes of schizoaffective disorder.

Stress management, therefore, aims to reduce levels of stress so that it stops having negative effects on people's lives, rather than to eliminate it completely. Below are some suggestions for ways to manage stress.

Problem solving

Having a plan for solving problems can help to stop people feeling overwhelmed by their problems. Stress itself can make problems seem so much more problematic than they really are. There are certain steps involved in problem solving:

1. Identify the problem

2. Brainstorm all the possible solutions

3. Evaluate the different possible solutions

4. Select a solution

5. Plan the solution

6. Implement the plan

7. Evaluate the plan (did it work?)

8. Praise and encourage yourself

Taking time out

A major part of reducing stress is about balance between things that relieve stress and things that provide people with stimulation. This translates into doing things like watching TV or reading a book after doing something that is more challenging such as filling in accounts or an important form. Doing something enjoyable can also help to lift people's spirits when they feel stressed.

Self-expression

People can use forms of self-expression such as writing a journal, painting, sculpture, poetry and music to help to reduce the effects of distressing thoughts and feelings.

Relaxation techniques

Relaxation techniques can be hugely beneficial in controlling stress for people with schizoaffective disorder. There are a number of different types of relaxation techniques. People should try out the different techniques to find the ones that work best for them.

- Breathing relaxation

- Progressive relaxation

- Autogenic relaxation

- Imagery or visualisation relaxation

Healthy diet

It is important for people with schizoaffective disorder to have a healthy diet. As a general rule, this means having foods from all five food groups every day. This includes:

- Breads and cereals

- Fruit

- Vegetables

- Meat, fish or poultry

- Milk or milk products such as cheese and yoghurt

There appears to be a link between food and the symptoms of schizoaffective disorder, although research is only in its infancy with regard to the exact foods that may worsen or improve symptoms of mood and psychotic disorders. Some people have found that limiting their intake of gluten and carbohydrates have resulted in an improvement in psychotic symptoms.

A diet high in omega-3 fatty acids, found in foods such as salmon, mackerel and sardines can help both mood and psychotic symptoms in people with schizoaffective disorder. Additionally, the folic acid that is found in green leafy vegetables may help people with depressive symptoms that don't respond well to treatment.

Avoiding bad habits

Avoiding substances that can make symptoms worse is another way that people with schizoaffective disorder can help control their condition.

Smoking

Smoking is a common bad habit for people with schizoaffective disorder. This is because nicotine can have an anxiety reducing effect and therefore cigarettes are often used as a form of self-medication. The potential damaging effects of nicotine, however, outweigh the benefits and smoking is a bad habit that should be avoided.

Caffeine

People with schizoaffective disorder tend to have a very high caffeine intake. High levels of caffeine can be damaging and can lead to caffeine intoxication. The symptoms of caffeine intoxication are:

- Nervousness
- Restlessness
- Insomnia
- Excitement
- Rapid heartbeat
- Muscle twitching

Caffeine can also worsen symptoms for people with schizoaffective disorder and can interfere with the efficiency of medication used to treat the illness.

Alcohol and street drugs

Alcohol and street drug abuse is a big problem for people with schizoaffective disorder. In addition to the negative effects of substance abuse experienced by the general population, people with schizoaffective disorder who abuse alcohol and drugs tend to have more symptoms and a much higher rate of relapse.

The odd social drink is okay for most people with schizoaffective disorder, but heavy alcohol consumption should be avoided. Street drugs should always be avoided as these can trigger psychotic episodes for people with schizoaffective disorder.

Accepting the illness

Many people with schizoaffective disorder struggle to come to terms with their diagnosis. They don't like accepting that they have a lifelong illness, or that they may have to take medication for the foreseeable future.

Accepting that they have an illness is an important step for people with schizoaffective disorder in taking back some control. It is important not to reject or underestimate the illness, and people shouldn't try to carry on as though they haven't got the illness. Taking that kind of approach can only make symptoms worse in the long run. Instead, it is much more beneficial to accept the illness and concentrate on learning how to manage symptoms and prevent or reduce the number of future relapses.

Chapter Thirteen: Managing Mood Symptoms

When people are first diagnosed with schizoaffective disorder, they can feel quite overwhelmed by their mood symptoms. It may seem as though their symptoms are in control of them, and if the person has been experiencing symptoms for a while they may think that their symptoms are impossible to manage.

This chapter looks at ways in which people can manage the symptoms of mood disorder in schizoaffective disorder, including:

- Keeping a mood chart
- Maintaining regular routines
- Dealing with mania
- Dealing with depression
- Dealing with suicidal thoughts and feelings

Keeping a mood chart

Many people with schizoaffective disorder find it helpful to keep a mood chart that records their mood symptoms as well as things such as anxiety, irritability, suicidal thoughts and impulses, psychotic symptoms and changes in sleep patterns.

There is an example of a mood chart below and a blank copy in Appendix Three. The chart contains space to record information for an entire month on a single page. It can be useful for people with schizoaffective disorder to share their mood chart with their psychiatrist and other mental health professionals involved in their care.

Rating mood

The mood section of the chart has sections labels depressed, normal and elevated. People should rate their mood from -3 (severe depression) to -1 (mild depression) under the depressed heading, and +1 (mild mania/hypomania) to +3 (severe mania) under the elevated heading.

Other symptoms

There is also space on the mood chart to note down symptoms such as anxiety, irritability, suicidal thoughts and psychotic symptoms. People should rate these additional symptoms from 0 (no symptoms) to 3 (severe symptoms).

Sleep

Recording the number of hours of sleep they get is important for people with schizoaffective disorder as changes in sleeping patterns can have an impact on their mood symptoms.

Figure 13.1: Sample mood chart

Day	Depressed			Normal	Elevated				Irritability	Psychosis	Suicidality	Sleep
	-3	-2	-1	0	+1	+2	+3	Anxiety				

1	√								3	3	1	1	9
2	√								3	3	1	1	9
3	√								3	3	1	1	9
4	√								3	3	1	1	9
5		√							3	3	1	0	9
6		√							2	3	1	0	9
7		√							2	3	1	0	9
8		√							2	3	1	0	9
9		√							2	3	1	0	9
10		√							2	2	1	0	8
11		√							2	2	1	0	8
12		√							2	2	1	0	8
13		√							2	2	1	0	8
14		√							3	2	1	0	8
15		√							3	2	1	0	8
16			√						1	2	1	0	8
17			√						0	0	1	0	6
18			√						0	0	1	0	6
19			√						0	0	1	0	6
20			√						0	0	1	0	6

Maintaining regular routines

People with schizoaffective disorder may find that their moods are affected by patterns of everyday activity, such as falling asleep, waking up, having meals and social interaction. These kinds of activities set what is called the body clock and it is important for people to have regular routines in order to avoid triggering symptoms of their mood disorder.

Keeping a record of activity can also help people to identify the relationship between symptoms and changes in daily routines. Over a period of weeks and months, people tend to see certain patterns emerging that can help them to manage their illness better.

There is an example of a mood and activity chart below and a blank copy in Appendix Four. The chart contains space to record mood, irritability, anxiety and psychotic symptoms as well as daily activity, hours of sleep, any triggers and notes and observations.

Figure 13.2: Sample mood and activity chart

	Monday	Tuesday
Mood	-2	-3
Irritability	1	2
Anxiety	2	3
Psychosis	2	3
Morning	Ate breakfast alone	Woke up early
	Slept	Went for a walk – agitated
	Had lunch	Skipped lunch
Afternoon	Went for a walk	Tried to read
	Had dinner	Had dinner
	Watched TV	Bed early
	Bed	
Evening		
Triggers	None	Less sleep
Hours Slept	9	6

Dealing with mania

Mania, in its most severe forms, can be extremely damaging, affecting finances, relationships, employment and even causing legal problems. Although mania can feel exhilarating at the time, the problems that accompany manic episodes are far reaching and long lasting. Some people miss their mania when they are well or depressed, but this is a dangerous mind set to fall into.

It is impossible to fully prevent future manic or hypomanic episodes, but there are steps that people can take to manage mania. This involves making a plan to recognise signs and symptoms of illness and how best to deal with them when they occur.

Relapse plans

Relapse plans should be made when the person is well, and should contain details of what symptoms to look out for, what to do when the symptoms occur, and what other people can do to help. There are three stages to creating a relapse plan for mania:

1. Identify warning signs (sometimes called prodromal symptoms)

2. List preventative measures (what to do to stall the symptoms of impending mania)

3. Create a written plan detailing warning signs and preventative measures

In the first stage, people should make a list of early warning signs that herald the beginning of a hypomanic or manic episode. In identifying early warning signs, people should also identify situations that may trigger symptoms.

In the second stage, people should list actions that they, or others, should take if they notice that some of their warning signs are happening.

The tables below and the worksheets in Appendix Five should help people to identify their warning signs and preventative measures and help them to draw up their relapse plan.

Figure 13.3: Identifying early warning (prodromal) symptoms

	Examples
Describe what the mood is like when becoming manic or hypomanic	Happy, more aware, irritable, euphoric, anxious, wired, excitable
Describe any changes in activity and energy levels when becoming manic or hypomanic	Taking on lots of new projects, talking more, talking faster.
Describe changes in thinking and perception when becoming manic or hypomanic	Thoughts race, sounds get louder, colours get brighter, I think I can do anything
Describe changes in sleeping pattern when becoming	Sleeping less than normal but not feeling tired, staying up later, waking earlier

manic or hypomanic	
Describe the things that you do when becoming manic or hypomanic that you wouldn't do normally	Spending too much money, gambling, driving recklessly, sleeping with lots of different people
Describe the context of some past hypomanic or manic episodes	Increase in working hours, stopping medication, stressful situations, increase in family commitments or conflicts

Figure 13.4: Preventative steps for mania

(The following are some suggestions for preventative measures. It is best for people to think up their own preventative measures if their warning symptoms aren't covered here)

If you _____ when becoming manic or hypomanic...	You could....
Tend to spend or gamble money recklessly	Give credit cards to someone else to look after Keep only the minimum amount of money in easily accessible bank accounts Stay away from shopping

	centres or casinos
	Avoiding making any kind of investments
	Avoid online shopping
	Apply the 48 hour rule (see below)
Tend to drive recklessly	Give the car keys to someone else for safekeeping
	Let other people drive you around
Tend to make risky decisions and have grandiose plans	Make a contract with yourself not to make any major decisions when manic
	Talk any major decisions over with other people
	Apply the 48 hour rule (see below)
Find yourself sleeping much less than normal	Talk to your doctor about using a sleeping tablet temporarily in order to maintain a regular sleeping pattern
If you feel as though you are going manic	Talk to your doctor or other mental health professional
	Increase dosage of medication to an agreed level

Writing down a relapse plan

If people follow steps one and two above, they should have the required information needed to draw up their relapse contract.

Figure 13.5: Sample relapse plan

Name	Joe Blogs
Doctor's Name:	Dr Smith
Doctor's Telephone Number:	01234 567890
Early warning signs of mania of hypomania	Feeling giddy and excitable Not sleeping much and waking up full of energy Spending money recklessly on credit cards Having lots of plans Driving too fast Sleeping with lots of different people
Circumstances when the symptoms tend to occur	Having to work late Increased stress at work Conflict with family
Other warning signs noticed by others	Talking much more than normal
Preventative measures for early warning signs	Taking extra medication Taking a sleeping tablet Giving credit and debit cards to mum to look after

	Giving car keys to dad to look after
Preventative measures other people can help with	Not inviting me out drinking
	Talking me out of extravagant plans

The 48 hour rule

Some people with schizoaffective disorder use what is called the 48 hour rule when they are manic. This means that a person should wait 24 hours after two good nights' sleep before making any major decisions or purchases. During the 48 hours, they should discuss the intended purchase or decision with as many trusted people as they can. They should also ask themselves:

- If someone else wanted to do this, what would I advise them to do?

- What is the worst thing that could happen if I don't do this?

- What is the worst thing that could happen if I do do this?

Dealing with depression

People with schizoaffective disorder tend to experience depression very intensely and therefore it is important for them to learn to recognise their warning signs. It can also be helpful to learn cognitive behavioural techniques for dealing with the negative thought processes involved with depressive thinking.

Identifying warning signs

As with mania, it is helpful for people to draw up a list of their warning signs of depression, so that they can take action to try and stop depressive episodes in their tracks.

The table below and the blank worksheet in Appendix Six should help people with schizoaffective disorder to identify their warning signs of impending depressive episodes.

Figure 13.6: Identifying warning signs of depression

	Examples
Describe what your mood is like when you are becoming depressed:	Sad, anxious, irritable, nervous, flat, numb, restless
Describe what changes there are in your activity and energy levels when you are becoming depressed:	Feeling slowed down, withdrawing from people, feeling tired, doing less
Describe what changes there are in your thinking and perception when you are becoming depressed:	Can't get interested in things, feel self-critical, feel guilty, feel hopeless, can't make decisions
Describe what changes there are in your sleeping patterns when you are becoming depressed	Wanting to sleep more, waking up in the middle of the night
Describe anything else that seems different when you are becoming depressed.	

Preventative measures for depression

There are fewer things that people can do to stop episodes of depression, but some suggestions are:

- Increasing or starting anti-depressant medication

- Try to keep active, doing one or two things that you usually enjoy

- Talk to trusted friends and family

- Talk to your psychiatrist or other mental health professional

- Use cognitive behavioural techniques (see below) to combat negative thinking which contributes to depression

Cognitive behavioural approaches to depression

When people are depressed, they tend to think very negatively. Therapists may refer to this as negative cognitions. People with schizoaffective disorder who are experiencing an episode of depression tend to have very negative beliefs about themselves, such as 'I'm no good', and about their future, such as 'nothing good is ever going to happen to me'.

Cognitive behavioural therapy assumes that negative automatic thoughts are provoked by certain events and these negative thoughts reflect the negative core beliefs that the person has about themselves. These are both major contributory factors in depressed mood. Cognitive behavioural therapy aims to find alternative ways of thinking that don't focus on negativity.

The most effective way of challenging negative thoughts and beliefs is to use a thought record sheet. See below for an example and Appendix Seven for a blank copy of the thought record sheet.

The thought record asks people to identify situations that have prompted negative automatic thoughts and then record the situation, the emotions the situation brought about and the automatic thoughts the situation generated (columns 1-3). The record sheet then asks the person to find evidence both for and against the negative automatic thought, and to then record an alternative or balanced thought that replaces the original negative thoughts.

Completing thought record sheets can be challenging for people with depression, but nevertheless they are very useful in helping to combat the negative thinking that contributes so strongly to depression.

Figure 13.7: Thought record sheet

Situation	Emotions – Rate intensity 0-100%	Automatic Thoughts	Evidence		Alternative/ Balanced Thoughts
			For	Against	
Simon said he would call me back but he didn't	Upset 100% Depressed 100%	I'm not important to him or anyone else I'm worthless No one wants to bother with me any more No one cares about me	This is the second time that Simon hasn't called me back I'm no fun to be around any more Other people have 'forgotten' to call me back	Simon has just got a promotion at work and I suppose he could have forgotten to call me back I can't expect everyone just to drop everything and call me I've forgotten to call people back in the past and it doesn't mean that I don't care about the person	Okay, so Simon forgot to call me back, but he could be busy and it's very easy to forget to return a call – I've done the same. Just because he didn't call it doesn't mean that he doesn't care.

Dealing with suicidal thoughts

When people with schizoaffective disorder are depressed, it is common for them to have thoughts about ending their lives. They may also feel suicidal because of psychotic symptoms. Additionally, some people with schizoaffective disorder may feel suicidal even when they are not depressed or psychotic. This is called chronic suicidality.

People with schizoaffective disorder have a much higher risk of committing suicide than the general population. Between 30% and 40% of people with schizoaffective disorder will attempt suicide at some point. 10% of them succeed in ending their lives. Suicidal thoughts are a tragic part of schizoaffective disorder. Virtually everyone with schizoaffective disorder will experience suicidal thoughts at some point during the course of the illness.

Suicide prevention

The crux of suicide prevention is decreasing or removing access to the means a person has of committing suicide and increasing support from mental health professionals, family and friends.

The first stage in suicide prevention, then, is getting rid of, or putting out of reach, the things that people may use to kill themselves. These include:

- Sleeping pills
- Other medications
- Poisons
- Ropes
- Sharp knives

To avoid the risk of overdose when suicidal, it is often best for people to keep only a couple of day's supply of medication in the house and have someone else take care of the rest.

These steps, of course, only get rid of the means of suicide, not the intentions, but in fact this greatly decreases the chance that someone will kill themselves.

The second stage of suicide prevention is for a person to see their psychiatrist or other mental health professional immediately, or at the very least talk to someone, so that the doctor knows that the person is at risk.

A third stage of suicide prevention is for a person to review their reasons for living. This is a list of reasons why a person should want to live instead of die. It is helpful to draw up this list whilst they are well so that they have it on hand if they begin to feel suicidal. The list could include things such as:

- I have plans for the future that I am looking forward to
- My family loves and supports me
- It would hurt my family and friends if I was to die
- I want to watch my children/ grandchildren grow up
- There are so many experiences I haven't had yet

Chapter Fourteen: Managing Psychotic Symptoms

When people are first diagnosed with schizoaffective disorder, they can feel quite overwhelmed by their psychotic symptoms. It may seem as though their symptoms are in control of them, and if the people has been experiencing symptoms for a while they may feel as though their symptoms are impossible to manage.

This chapter looks at ways in which people can manage psychotic symptoms in schizoaffective disorder, including:

- Coping with hallucinations and delusions

- Cognitive therapy for hallucinations and delusions

- Preparing for relapse

Coping with hallucinations and delusions

Hallucinations can be incredibly difficult to live with, particularly if they are voices that are harsh and critical towards the person experiencing them.

Delusions, similarly, can be very difficult to deal with because when a person is delusional, they wholeheartedly believe the delusions to be true. It is therefore almost impossible to challenge the delusions.

There are, however, strategies that people can use to help deal with their hallucinations and delusions.

Basic coping strategies

Below is a list of strategies that people with schizoaffective disorder have found to be helpful in coping with hallucinations and delusions:

- Humming

- Listening to music
- Praying
- Meditation
- Using a mantra
- Painting
- Imagery
- Going for a walk
- Phoning a friend
- Exercising
- Using relaxation techniques
- Doing yoga
- Watching TV
- Doing crosswords or other puzzles
- Trying a new hobby
- Playing a computer game
- Calling a mental health professional
- Taking a warm bath
- Reminding yourself that you're safe
- Reminding yourself that you don't need to obey any voices you hear
- Role playing for and against voices
- Listing evidence for and against the delusional belief
- Listing evidence for and against what the voices are saying
- Counting backwards from 100 in 3s

- Calling a support/ crisis line
- Talking to people you trust

Cognitive therapy for hallucinations and delusions

Cognitive behavioural approaches to hallucinations

In Chapter Eleven, we looked at cognitive behavioural therapy for schizoaffective disorder. You may remember the acronym ACT:

- A = activating event
- B = belief about the event
- C = consequence – feelings and behaviours

The ABC approach can be a useful method of coping with the distress that hallucinations cause. It can be helpful to record the ABCs of triggering situations in order to understand where thoughts and feelings about hallucinations come from. People can use the table below, and the blank worksheet in Appendix Eight, to help them record the ABCs of triggering situations.

Figure 14.1: ABC for hallucinations – example

Activating event	Belief about the event	Consequences
If voices: How many? How loud? How often? What triggers them? What does it/ they say? Other hallucinations: vision, smell, physical sensation	What goes through your mind? Do you agree? If it was true/false, what would it mean to you? What would be the worst thing about that? How powerful is the voice? How much control do you have? How do you explain it? Who is it? What does it want? How are you making sense of it all? What does it all mean?	How do you feel? What do you feel like doing? What do you do?
Three voices shouting loudly at me, telling me that I should kill myself because I'm not worthy of being alive	What if they're right? I'm not worthy of being alive. The voices are more powerful than I am. They seem to know better than I do. The voices are the voices of angels, messengers of God and of course they must be right	Scared, worried. I think that I should maybe find some way of killing myself, but I'm not sure how to do it.

Cognitive behavioural approaches to delusions

Cognitive behavioural approaches to delusions, particularly paranoid delusions, use the same ABC method as cognitive behavioural approaches to hallucinations. The

ABC method for delusions looks at how certain events can trigger delusional thoughts and feelings, and can help to reduce the distress associated with delusional beliefs about events.

People can use the table below and the blank worksheet in Appendix Nine to help them record the ABCs of triggering situations.

Figure 14.2: ABCs for delusions

Activating event	Belief about the event	Consequences
When? Where? Who with? What happened? Who said or did what? What did you sense?	What went through your mind? If that was true/false, what would it mean to you? What would be the worst thing about that? How much do you believe this thought (rate from 0-100%)	
There was a series of supposed wrong number phone calls to my mobile over a period of several days.	MI5 are checking up on me. They're using my mobile phone to track where I am and what I'm doing and the calls were to make sure that I still had the phone and hadn't sold it on to someone else. Belief rating 100%	I felt frightened and intimidated – which is how they wanted me to feel. To outfox them, though, I threw my phone into the river so they couldn't use it to track me down any more.

Cognitive behavioural approaches to hallucinations and delusions

In chapter thirteen, we looked at thought record sheets for dealing with negative automatic thoughts in depression.

Like the ABC worksheets, thought record worksheets can also be useful for trying to challenge the thoughts and feelings that accompany hallucinations and delusions. There is an example of a thought record sheet for delusions and hallucinations below and a blank copy in Appendix Seven.

Figure 14.3: Thought record sheet for hallucinations and delusions

Situat-ion	Emotion – Rate intensity 0-100%	Automatic Thoughts	Evidence		Alternative/ Balanced Thoughts
			For	Against	
There was a series of wrong number phone calls to my mobile phone over a period of several days	Fear 100% Anger 85%	MI5 are tracking my movem-ents through my mobile phone	The phone calls were all from a withheld number I've felt as though I've been watched for a while	People do dial the wrong number sometime s – I've done it myself	Although it's possible that MI5 were using my phone to track me, it's also possible that the phone calls might have been genuine wrong number phone calls

Preparing for relapse

Relapse in schizoaffective disorder is something that cannot be entirely eliminated even with the use of medication and therapy. It is relatively common, then, for people with schizoaffective disorder to experience recurrences of their psychotic symptoms. Because of this, it is necessary for them to be prepared for relapses and to learn to recognise early warning signs.

It is helpful for people with schizoaffective disorder to have a relapse plan for their psychotic symptoms, which should list the early warning symptoms and strategies to put in place when the symptoms occur.

Identifying early warning signs of psychosis

Although everybody's experience of psychosis is personal to them, there are a number of early warning signs that are quite common. People creating a relapse plan should select from the list below the symptoms that they have experienced in past psychotic episodes, or leading up to past psychotic episodes, and add any symptoms they've experienced that aren't listed here.

Early warning signs of psychotic relapse
Thinking and perceptions

- Thoughts are racing

- Senses seem sharper

- Thinking I have special powers

- Thinking I can read other people's minds

- Thinking that other people can read my mind

- Receiving personal messages from the TV or radio

- Having difficulty making decisions

- Experiencing strange sensations

- Being preoccupied by things

- Thinking that I am somebody else

- Seeing visions or things that other people can't see

- Thinking people are talking about me

- Thinking people are against me
- Having more nightmares
- Having difficulty concentrating
- Thinking bizarre things
- Thinking my thoughts are being controlled by someone/ something else
- Hearing voices
- Thinking that a part of me has changed shape

Feelings

- Feeling helpless or useless
- Feeling afraid of going crazy
- Feeling anxious and restless
- Feeling increasingly religious
- Feeling like I'm being watched
- Feeling isolated
- Feeling tired or lacking energy
- Feeling confused or puzzled
- Feeling forgetful or distant
- Feeling as though I'm in another world
- Feeling strong and powerful
- Feeling unable to cope with everyday tasks
- Feeling like I'm being punished
- Feeling like I can't trust other people
- Feeling irritable

- Feeling guilty

Behaviours

- Difficulty sleeping
- Speech comes out jumbled or filled with odd words
- Talking or smiling to myself
- Acting suspiciously as if being watched
- Behaving oddly for no reason
- Spending time alone
- Neglecting my appearance
- Acting like I am someone else
- Not seeing people
- Not eating
- Not leaving the house
- Behaving like a child
- Refusing to do simple requests
- Drinking more
- Smoking more
- Unable to sit still for long
- Behaving aggressively

Identifying strategies for coping with symptoms

The next stage of creating a relapse plan for psychotic symptoms in schizoaffective disorder is the identification of things that can be done to deal with the symptoms when they occur. These can be things like:

- Meditation

- Yoga

- Going for a walk

- Distraction techniques such as

    o Listening to music

    o Counting backwards in 3s from 100

    o Listening to guided imagery CDs

- Contacting a mental health professional to discuss symptoms

- Taking an agreed extra dose of antipsychotic medication (this should be discussed in advance with the psychiatrist or GP)

- Increasing medication to an agreed higher dosage (again, this should be discussed in advance with the psychiatrist or GP)

- Attending a day clinic

- Phoning a crisis line

- Using CBT techniques to cope with hallucinations and delusions

- Hospitalisation

Putting it all together: the relapse plan for psychotic symptoms

Once stages one and two of the relapse plan strategy have been completed, it is possible to put together a written plan that details warning signs and coping strategies as well as important contact details for use in a crisis.

There is an example of a relapse plan below and a blank
worksheet in Appendix Ten.

Figure 14.4: Relapse plan for psychosis

Name:	Joe Blogs
Date:	1/1/2010
Early warning signs: (list in ascending order of severity)	Thoughts are racing Senses seem sharper Thinking I can read other people's minds Experiencing strange sensations Thinking people are talking about me Seeing things that other people can't see Hearing voices
Action plan: (list strategies for coping)	Do yoga Meditation Distraction techniques Call mental health team Take an extra dose of medication Increase Quetiapine to 600mg See Dr Smith more regularly Agree to hospitalisation if symptoms deteriorate
Important contacts: Mental health team:	

Crisis team:	
Mental Health Support Line:	
Psychiatrist:	
GP:	

Chapter Fifteen: Advice for Friends and Family

Schizoaffective disorder doesn't just affect the person with the illness – it also affects the lives of the people who care about them – their family and friends. This chapter looks at the ways people can learn to cope if their friend or close relative has schizoaffective disorder and what they can do to help.

Getting help for a loved one

If someone thinks that a friend or family member might be experiencing the symptoms of schizoaffective disorder, they may find it hard to get help. This is often the case when the person they are concerned about doesn't realise that they are unwell and therefore refuses to accept that they need help. This might be because the delusions the person is experiencing makes them think that their problems are caused by aliens, for example, or they may not accept that they have a problem at all, particularly if they are experiencing mania.

If the person who is ill poses no risk to themselves or others, and their health is not deteriorating to the point where they are neglecting themselves, it is reasonable to wait and then try repeatedly, but gently, to get them to see a doctor. Furthermore, it is important to try to avoid pressurising the person – and it is imperative not to try to trick them into seeing a psychiatrist because then they will become suspicious of any other attempts to help them.

However, if a loved one seems to be suicidal or their behaviour poses a threat to themselves or other people, and they still refuse to accept help, then it may be necessary for them to be committed to a psychiatric hospital for treatment. It is very difficult to have a person committed for treatment unless they pose a significant risk to themselves and others.

In the United States, there are two kinds of commitment: emergency and long term. In many states, any person can initiate a petition for emergency commitment. The person initiating the petition asks a doctor to examine the unwell person – some states require two doctors. The examination may take place anywhere. An emergency commitment lasts for 72 hours in most states.

In the United Kingdom, there are three main types of compulsory detention, known as Sections of the Mental Health Act (2007):

- Section 4: Admission for assessment in cases of emergency – up to 72 hours maximum. The person needs to be assessed by one doctor, and evidence must be provided that the admission is a matter of emergency and absolutely necessary.

- Section 2: Admission for assessment – up to 28 days maximum. The person needs to be assessed by two medical professionals, one of which should be a psychiatrist

- Section 3: Admission for treatment – up to 6 months, renewable after 6 months and subsequently for one year at a time

Caring for carers

Caring for someone with schizoaffective disorder can cause significant amounts of stress. It can also be an isolating experience, especially if the carer doesn't have a good support system themselves. For this reason, many community mental health teams in the United Kingdom offer a carer's assessment of need. This is done by specially trained carer support workers. Carer support workers can offer the help and support that carers desperately need. They offer a chance for carers to discuss problems, concerns and worries and may liaise with other members of the community mental health team treating the person with schizoaffective disorder.

Coping strategies

There are a number of strategies that carers can use to help them cope when someone they love has schizoaffective disorder.

Knowledge

Learning about the illness and what to expect is an important part of learning to cope with schizoaffective disorder. Knowing what they are dealing with can make the illness more manageable. Also, knowing what to look out for in the person they care for – the person's early warning signs – can help to stop episodes of illness in their tracks.

Acceptance

Just as it is important for people with schizoaffective disorder to accept their illness, it is equally important for carers, friends and family to accept that their loved one has the illness. Acceptance is the first step to adapting to the changes that may be necessary because of the illness. Understanding that schizoaffective disorder is a recurrent illness can help friends and relatives to accept the disorder. Realising that schizoaffective disorder is treatable and manageable can also help with acceptance.

Having healthy boundaries

It is important for people who care for someone with schizoaffective disorder to remember to maintain healthy boundaries between them and the person that they care for. Some things that carers can do to maintain healthy boundaries are;

- Acknowledging that the carer has feelings and needs as well as the person with the illness

- Being prepared to delegate caring responsibilities to other family members

- Arranging to have time to themselves

- Taking care of their own health

- Finding someone to talk to or joining a carers' support group

- Trying not to get over involved

- Not expecting to be able to fix everything

What to say to someone who is deluded or hallucinating

It is important not to minimise or dismiss such symptoms as delusions or hallucinations, or try to argue the person out of them by pointing out the illogicality of what they are saying. It is best to respect what the person is saying or experiencing, without colluding with it. For example, a carer might say to the person who is ill, 'I understand that you believe that people are talking about you and that someone is plotting against you. That must be very frightening for you, and I can understand and sympathise, although we must agree to differ about whether it is true.'

Encouraging people with schizoaffective disorder to take medication

The chances of schizoaffective disorder getting worse, or of a relapse occurring, are more than halved in most cases if the person with the illness continues to take long term medication. Their family and friends may be in the best position to make sure the person actually takes their medication, especially since side effects might put the person off taking his or her medication.

Avoiding criticism or over-involvement

People with schizoaffective disorder often need space and time alone, and may sometimes find it difficult to play a full role in family life. Carers, family and friends should avoid criticising the person with the illness as this can put the person under pressure and increase the risk of relapse. It is also best to avoid too much expressed emotion, including not just critical comments, but also over-protectiveness and smothering.

Appendix One: DSM-IV (TR) Criterion for Schizoaffective Disorder

A. An uninterrupted period of illness during which, at some time, there is either (1) a Major Depressive Episode, (2) a Manic Episode, or (3) a Mixed Episode concurrent with symptoms that meet (4) Criterion A for Schizophrenia.

Note: The Major Depressive Episode must include depressed mood.

(1) Criteria for Major Depressive Episode

o Five (or more) of the following symptoms have been present during the same 2-week period and represent a change from previous functioning; at least one of the symptoms is either (1) depressed mood or (2) loss of interest or pleasure.

Note: Do not include symptoms that are clearly due to a general medical condition, or mood-incongruent delusions or hallucinations.

1. depressed mood most of the day, nearly every day, as indicated by either subjective report (e.g., feels sad or empty) or observation made by others (e.g., appears tearful). **Note:** In children and adolescents, can be irritable mood.

2. markedly diminished interest or pleasure in all, or almost all, activities most of the day, nearly every day (as indicated by either

subjective account or observation
made by others)

3. significant weight loss when not
dieting or weight gain (e.g., a
change of more than 5% of body
weight in a month), or decrease or
increase in appetite nearly every
day. **Note:** In children, consider
failure to make expected weight
gains.

4. insomnia or hypersomnia nearly
every day

5. psychomotor agitation or
retardation nearly every day
(observable by others, not merely
subjective feelings of restlessness
or being slowed down)

6. fatigue or loss of energy nearly
every day

7. feelings of worthlessness or
excessive or inappropriate guilt
(which may be delusional) nearly
every day (not merely self-reproach
or guilt about being sick)

8. diminished ability to think or
concentrate, or indecisiveness,
nearly every day (either by
subjective account or as observed
by others)

9. recurrent thoughts of death (not just
fear of dying), recurrent suicidal
ideation without a specific plan, or a

suicide attempt or a specific plan for committing suicide

o The symptoms do not meet criteria for a Mixed Episode

o The symptoms cause clinically significant distress or impairment in social, occupational, or other important areas of functioning.

o The symptoms are not due to the direct physiological effects of a substance (e.g., a drug of abuse, a medication) or a general medical condition (e.g., hypothyroidism).

o The symptoms are not better accounted for by Bereavement, i.e., after the loss of a loved one, the symptoms persist for longer than 2 months or are characterized by marked functional impairment, morbid preoccupation with worthlessness, suicidal ideation, psychotic symptoms, or psychomotor retardation.

(2) Criteria for Manic Episode

o A distinct period of abnormally and persistently elevated, expansive, or irritable mood, lasting at least 1 week (or any duration if hospitalization is necessary).

o During the period of mood disturbance, three (or more) of the following symptoms have persisted (four if the mood is only irritable) and have been present to a significant degree:

1. inflated self-esteem or grandiosity

2. decreased need for sleep (e.g., feels rested after only 3 hours of sleep)

3. more talkative than usual or pressure to keep talking

4. flight of ideas or subjective experience that thoughts are racing

5. distractibility (i.e., attention too easily drawn to unimportant or irrelevant external stimuli)

6. increase in goal-directed activity (either socially, at work or school, or sexually) or psychomotor agitation

7. excessive involvement in pleasurable activities that have a high potential for painful consequences (e.g., engaging in unrestrained buying sprees, sexual indiscretions, or foolish business investments)

o The symptoms do not meet criteria for a Mixed Episode

o The mood disturbance is sufficiently severe to cause marked impairment in occupational functioning or in usual social activities or relationships with others, or to necessitate hospitalization to prevent harm to self or others, or there are psychotic features.

o The symptoms are not due to the direct physiological effects of a substance (e.g., a drug of abuse, a medication, or other treatment) or a general medical condition (e.g., hyperthyroidism).

(3) Criteria for Mixed Episode

o The criteria are met both for a Manic Episode and for a Major Depressive Episode (except for duration) nearly every day during at least a 1-week period.

o The mood disturbance is sufficiently severe to cause marked impairment in occupational functioning or in usual social activities or relationships with others, or to necessitate hospitalization to prevent harm to self or others, or there are psychotic features.

o The symptoms are not due to the direct physiological effects of a substance (e.g., a drug of abuse, a medication, or other treatment) or a general medical condition (e.g., hyperthyroidism).

(4) Criterion A of Schizophrenia

o Two (or more) of the following, each present for a significant portion of time during a 1-month period (or less if successfully treated):

- delusions

- hallucinations

- disorganized speech (e.g., frequent derailment or incoherence)

- grossly disorganized or catatonic behaviour

- negative symptoms, i.e., affective flattening, alogia, or avolition

o Only one symptom is required if delusions are bizarre or hallucinations consist of a voice keeping up a running commentary on the person's behaviour or thoughts, or two or more voices conversing with each other.

During the same period of illness, there have been delusions or hallucinations for at least 2 weeks in the absence of prominent mood symptoms.

Symptoms that meet criteria for a mood episode are present for a substantial portion of the total duration of the active and residual periods of the illness.

The disturbance is not due to the direct physiological effects of a substance (e.g., a drug of abuse, a medication) or a general medical condition.

Specify type:

- **Bipolar Type:** if the disturbance includes a Manic or a Mixed Episode (or a Manic or a Mixed Episode and Major Depressive Episodes)

- **Depressive Type:** if the disturbance only includes Major Depressive Episodes

Appendix Two: ICD-10 Criterion for Schizoaffective Disorder

F25 Schizoaffective Disorder

These are episodic disorders in which both affective and schizophrenic symptoms are prominent within the same episode of illness, preferably simultaneously, but at least within a few days of each other. Their relationship to typical mood (affective) disorders and to schizophrenic disorders is uncertain. They are given a separate category because they are too common to be ignored. Other conditions in which affective symptoms are superimposed upon or form part of a pre-existing schizophrenic illness, or in which they coexist or alternate with other types of persistent delusional disorders, are classified under the appropriate category. Mood-incongruent delusions or hallucinations in affective disorders do not by themselves justify a diagnosis of schizoaffective disorder.

Patients who suffer from recurrent schizoaffective episodes, particularly those whose symptoms are of the manic rather than the depressive type, usually make a full recovery and only rarely develop a defect state.

Diagnostic Guidelines

A diagnosis of schizoaffective disorder should be made only when both definite schizophrenic and definite affective symptoms are prominent simultaneously, or within a few days of each other, within the same episode of illness, and when, as a consequence of this, the episode of illness does not meet criteria for either schizophrenia or a depressive or manic episode. The term should not be applied to patients who exhibit schizophrenic symptoms and affective symptoms only in different episodes of illness. It is common, for example, for a schizophrenic patient to present with depressive symptoms in the aftermath of a psychotic episode (see post-schizophrenic depression). Some patients have recurrent schizoaffective episodes, which may be of the manic or depressive type or a mixture of the two. Others have one or two schizoaffective episodes interspersed between typical episodes of mania or depression. In the former case, schizoaffective disorder is the appropriate diagnosis. In the latter, the occurrence of an occasional schizoaffective episode does not invalidate a diagnosis of bipolar affective disorder or recurrent depressive disorder if the clinical picture is typical in other respects.

F25.0 Schizoaffective Disorder, Manic Type

A disorder in which schizophrenic and manic symptoms are both prominent in the same episode of illness. The abnormality of mood usually takes the form of elation, accompanied by increased self-esteem and grandiose ideas, but sometimes excitement or irritability are more obvious and accompanied by aggressive behaviour and persecutory ideas. In both cases there is increased energy, over activity, impaired concentration, and a loss of normal social inhibition. Delusions of reference, grandeur, or persecution may be present, but other more typically schizophrenic symptoms are required to establish the diagnosis. People may insist, for example, that their thoughts are being broadcast or interfered with, or that alien forces are trying to control them, or they may report hearing voices of varied kinds or express bizarre delusional ideas that are not merely grandiose or persecutory. Careful questioning is often required to establish that an individual really is experiencing these morbid phenomena, and not merely joking or talking in metaphors. Schizoaffective disorders, manic type, are usually florid psychoses with an acute onset; although behaviour is often grossly disturbed, full recovery generally occurs within a few weeks.

Diagnostic Guidelines

There must be a prominent elevation of mood, or a less obvious elevation of mood combined with increased irritability or excitement. Within the same episode, at least one and preferably two typically schizophrenic symptoms (as specified for schizophrenia [F20], diagnostic guidelines (a) - (d)) should be clearly present.

This category should be used both for a single schizoaffective episode of the manic type and for a recurrent disorder in which the majority of episodes are schizoaffective, manic type.

F25.1 Schizoaffective Disorder, Depressive Type

A disorder in which schizophrenic and depressive symptoms are both prominent in the same episode of illness. Depression of mood is usually accompanied by several characteristic depressive symptoms or behavioural abnormalities such as retardation, insomnia, loss of energy, appetite or weight, reduction of normal interests, impairment of concentration, guilt, feelings of hopelessness, and suicidal thoughts. At the same time, or within the same episode, other more typically schizophrenic symptoms are present; patients may insist, for example, that their thoughts are being broadcast or interfered with, or that alien forces are trying to control them. They may be convinced that they are being spied upon or plotted against and this is not justified by their own behaviour. Voices may be heard that are not merely disparaging or condemnatory but that talk of killing the patient or discuss this behaviour between themselves. Schizoaffective episodes of the depressive type are usually less florid and alarming than schizoaffective episodes of the manic type, but they tend to last longer and the prognosis is less favourable.

Diagnostic Guidelines

There must be prominent depression, accompanied by at least two characteristic depressive symptoms or associated behavioural abnormalities as listed for the depressive episode; within the same episode, at least one and preferably two typically schizophrenic symptoms (as specified for schizophrenia), diagnostic guidelines (a)-(d) should be clearly present.

This category should be used both for a single schizoaffective episode, depressive type, and for a recurrent disorder in which the majority of episodes are schizoaffective, depressive type.

Appendix Three and Four: Mood/ Activity Chart

Day	Depressed			Normal 0	Elevated			Anxiety	Irritability	Psychosis	Suicidality	Sleep
	-3	-2	-1		+1	+2	+3					
1												
2												
3												
4												
5												
6												
7												
8												
9												
10												
11												
12												
13												
14												
15												
16												
17												
18												
19												
20												
21												
22												
23												
24												
25												
26												
27												
28												
29												
30												

	Monday	Tuesday	Wednesday	Thursday	Friday	Saturday	Sunday
Mood							
Irritability							
Anxiety							
Psychosis							
Morning Afternoon Evening							
Triggers							
Hours Slept							
Notes							

Appendix Five: Relapse Plan for Mania

Stage 1: Identifying early warning signs

Describe what the mood is like when becoming manic or hypomanic	
Describe any changes in activity and energy levels when becoming manic or hypomanic	
Describe changes in thinking and perception when becoming manic or hypomanic	
Describe changes in sleeping pattern when becoming manic or hypomanic	
Describe the things that you do when becoming manic or hypomanic that you wouldn't do normally	

Describe the context of some past hypomanic or manic episodes	

Stage 2: Identifying preventative measures

Manic/ Hypomanic symptom	Possible preventative measures

Stage 3: Creating a relapse plan

Name	
Doctor's Name:	
Doctor's Telephone No:	
Early warning signs of mania or hypomania	

Circumstances when the symptoms tend to occur	
Other warning signs noticed by others	
Preventative measures for early warning signs	
Preventative measures other people can help with	

Appendix Six: Warning Signs of Depression

Describe what your mood is like when you are becoming depressed:	
Describe what changes there are in your activity and energy levels when you are becoming depressed:	
Describe what changes there are in your thinking and perception when you are becoming depressed:	
Describe what changes there are in your sleeping patterns when you are becoming depressed	

Describe anything else that seems different when you are becoming depressed.	

Appendix Seven: Thought Record Sheet

Situation	Emotions – Rate intensity 0-100%	Automatic Thoughts	Evidence		Alternative/ Balanced Thoughts
			For	Against	

Appendix Eight: Cognitive Behavioural Approaches to Hallucinations

Activating event	Belief about the event	Consequences
If voices: How many? How loud? How often? What triggers them? What does it/ they say? Other hallucinations: vision, smell, physical sensation	What goes through your mind? Do you agree? If it was true/false, what would it mean to you? What would be the worst thing about that? How powerful is the voice? How much control do you have? How do you explain it? Who is it? What does it want? How are you making sense of it all? What does it all mean?	How do you feel? What do you feel like doing? What do you do?

Schizoaffective Disorder Simplified

Martine Daniel

Appendix Nine: Cognitive Behavioural Approached to Delusions

Activating event	Belief about the event	Consequences
When? Where? Who with? What happened? Who said or did what? What did you sense?	What went through your mind? If that was true/false, what would it mean to you? What would be the worst thing about that? How much do you believe this thought (rate from 0-100%)	

Schizoaffective Disorder Simplified

Appendix Ten: Relapse Plan for Psychosis

Name:	
Date:	
Early warning signs: (list in ascending order of severity)	
Action plan: (list strategies for coping)	

Important contacts: Mental health team: Crisis team: Mental Health Support Line: Psychiatrist: GP:	

Appendix Eleven: Resources

There are a number of mental health charities that can offer support and advice for people with schizoaffective disorder and their friends and families.

Rethink

Tel: 0845 456 0455
Website: www.rethink.org
Email: info@rethink.org

Rethink National Advice Service
Tel: 020 8974 6814 (open Mon-Fri, 10am-1pm)
Email: advice@rethink.org
Address: Rethink Advice, 15th Floor, 89 Albert Embankment, London, SE1 7TP

Mind

Mind*info*line

0845 766 0163
info@mind.org.uk

Mindinfoline
PO Box 277
Manchester
M60 3XN

Legal Advice Service

0845 2259393
legal@mind.org.uk

Mind LAS
PO Box 277

Manchester
M60 3XN

SANE

SANEline
0845 767 8000

SANEmail
http://www.sane.org.uk/SANEmail

Depression Alliance

Tel: 08451 232320
e-mail: information@depressionalliance.org
Website: www.depressionalliance.org

Depression UK (D-UK)

E-mail: info@depressionuk.org.uk
e-mail secretary: sec.duk@talktalk.net
Website: www.depressionuk.org.uk

Samaritans

Phone: 08457 90 90 90 (24-hour helpline)
Website: www.samaritans.org.uk

MDF: the bipolar organisation

Website: www.mdf.org.uk

Carers UK

Tel: 020 7490 8818

Carers line: 0808 808 7777

Email: info@carersuk.org

Website: www.carersuk.org

Mental Health Foundation

Tel: 020 7803 1101

Email: mhf@mhf.org.uk

Website: www.mentalhealth.org.uk

CPSIA information can be obtained at www.ICGtesting.com
Printed in the USA
BVOW08s0228010715

406943BV00001B/8/P